The Step-by-Step Guide to
Growing and Displaying
Roses

NELSON REGENCY
A Division of Thomas Nelson, Inc.

A NELSON/REGENCY BOOK

First published in 1994 by Thomas Nelson Publishers,
Nashville, Tennessee

Library of Congress Cataloguing in Publication Data
is available.

Library of Congress Card
93-083711

ISBN 0-8407-4244-4

Text by John Mattock, Peter McHoy and Jane Newdick
Edited by Gillian Haslam
Designed by Paul Turner and Sue Pressley,
Stonecastle Graphics Ltd
Photographs by Neil Sutherland, John Glover
and Peter McHoy
Typesetting by D.S.P.

Printed and bound in Hong Kong.

1 2 3 4 5 - - 98 97 96 95 94

CLB REF 4074

Introduction

The rose is a native of the temperate zones and thrives best given a cool, frosty winter, a mild spring, sun-filled summer days and a regular supply of water. However, it has also proved to be surprisingly versatile, tolerating a wide range of temperatures and variable amounts of sunlight and rainfall. In fact, as long as you avoid exposing roses to conditions of perpetual dry heat or prolonged intense cold, there are few places in the world where you cannot grow them.

Roses are found in a wide variety of colors and forms: wild roses add color to the countryside in early summer, sophisticated blooms grace the bride's wedding bouquet, and a wide range of cultivated varieties decorate our gardens. As well as the flowers of the rose, we can enjoy their beautiful, decorative hips in fall. Roses also vary tremendously in size, from the smallest miniature varieties currently enjoying enormous popularity to the vast ramblers that compete with other plants in the record books. The modern rose has been bred to withstand disease, to flower recurrently and to give pleasure not only as a garden plant, but also as a cut flower, bringing messages of love, hope and comfort. Even the smallest garden or town patio can find room for a rose bush, and the largest landscapes are enhanced by the eye-catching splashes of color provided by the world's most popular plant.

Tuscany Superb

The name is the sort that might be applied to a modern variety, but this Gallica rose with deep crimson-purple flowers was described over 140 years ago. The color of the blooms varies with age: they start deep crimson, but fade to purple. The yellow stamens contrast well with these dark petals, though they are often hidden by them. These very dark colors can look drab on a leafy bush in poor light, and the scent is poor.

Size Height: 5 ft. Spread: 3 ft.
Flowering Early and mid summer
Uses Borders
Scent Some scent

Tuscany Superb

The Prince

The Prince

Color is the outstanding feature of this fairly recently introduced New English rose. It opens deep crimson but soon changes to a remarkable royal purple. The blooms also have a very pleasing cupped rosette formation and of course that lovely old rose fragrance. The dark green foliage goes well with the flowers. The low height and bushy shape make it ideal for gardens too small to accommodate the larger traditional shrub roses.

Size Height: 2½ ft. Spread: 2½ ft.
Flowering Early to late summer
Uses Beds, borders
Scent Strong fragrance

Species Roses

Surprisingly, many of the ancestors of our familiar garden roses are still in existence, often still growing in their natural habitat. These original types are called species roses, the familiar wild roses that grow in our hedgerows. They include *Rosa virginiana* from North America, the dog rose, *R. canina,* from Europe and *R. chinensis* from the Far East. Species roses have only ever been discovered in the Northern Hemisphere and of the 120 different identifiable types, only 15–20 have ever contributed to the modern rose. We tend to think of the rose as being a development of western culture, but it is a fact that the modern rose would not exist if it had not been for the influx of breeding stock from the Middle and Far East. Many of the wild roses collected from their native habitat now play an important part in enhancing the beauty of our shrub borders. Many varieties have unique characteristics – colored foliage, an abundance of blossom, good plant shapes and a superb harvest of hips. They range in size from just 6 inches to 40 feet, require very little seasonal maintenance and, in addition, are virtually disease-free.

Right: *Rosa gallica* "Complicata" will develop into an enormous sprawling shrub 5 feet high and 10 feet across, with single, large flowers.

Left: *Rosa xanthina spontanea* "Canary Bird" is a slightly pendulous shrub that grows to 6 feet, with many yellow flowers in late spring.

3

Roseraie de l'Hay

One of the finest Rugosa hybrids, this beautiful plant has wine-purple elongated buds that open to crimson-purple blooms 4 inches across. It was raised at the beginning of the century by Jules Gravereaux, a passionate rosarian, who named it after a garden he created just south of Paris (it is still a famous rose garden). The scent is strong, and the plant flowers prolifically. The plant is densely clothed with tough, disease-resistant leaves, and it makes a good hedge.

Size   Height: 7 ft. Spread: 7 ft.
Flowering   Early and mid summer
Uses   Borders, hedge
Scent   Strong fragrance

Roseraie de l'Hay

Souvenir de Saint Anne's

Souvenir de Saint Anne's

This Bourbon rose is a sport (mutation) of "Souvenir de la Malmaison", which occurred in a garden at St. Anne's near Dublin. The flower is a delicate blush pink that fades almost to white. The pale, almost flimsy-looking blooms give the plant a delicate appearance, but actually it is tough and vigorous, producing its fragrant flowers prolifically, sometimes into early fall. Its pretty coloring and long flowering period make it attractive for the rose border.

Size   Height: 6 ft. Spread: 5 ft.
Flowering   Early to late summer
Uses   Borders
Scent   Strong fragrance

78

A Selection of Wild Rose Species

R. ecae var. "Helen Knight"
R. forrestiana
R. gallica "Complicata"
R. highdownensis
R. macrophylla
R. moyesii "Geranium"
R. omiensis pteracantha (sericia pteracantha)
R. pomifera (Apple Rose)
R. primula (Incense Rose)
R. roxburghii (Chestnut Rose)
R. glauca (rubrifolia)
R. rugosa alba
R. rugosa rubra
R. soulieana
R. sweginzowii
R. woodsii fendleri

The rugosa species make superb specimen plants for most gardens. They produce a spectacular harvest of large, tomato-shaped hips that attract birds in the fall.

Never prune or deadhead these plants. Pruning will result in stunted growth and no hips.

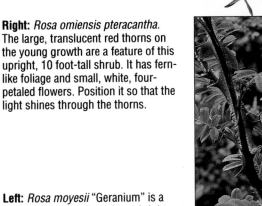

Right: *Rosa omiensis pteracantha.* The large, translucent red thorns on the young growth are a feature of this upright, 10 foot-tall shrub. It has fern-like foliage and small, white, four-petaled flowers. Position it so that the light shines through the thorns.

Left: *Rosa moyesii* "Geranium" is a 6 foot-tall rose that produces bright geranium red, single flowers, followed by bottle-shaped hips in the fall.

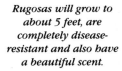

Above: *Rose rugosa* "Scabrosa" is the ideal rose for hedging, with the added bonus of beautiful, globular, red hips in fall. Rugosas are tolerant of practically any soil and appear proof against most common rose pests.

Rugosas will grow to about 5 feet, are completely disease-resistant and also have a beautiful scent.

Rosa rubrifolia

Most roses are grown for the beauty of the blooms alone, but this pretty species in renowned also for the unusual color of its gray-green foliage and purplish-red stems. The cerise-pink flowers are rather small, short-lived and unimpressive. Fall brings the bush to life again, however, with plentiful bunches of round, red hips. The stems are almost free of thorns, another advantage. You can keep it reasonably compact by regular pruning.

Size	Height: 6 ft. Spread: 5 ft.
Flowering	Early summer
Uses	Border, cutting (foliage)
Scent	No scent

Rosa rubrifolia

Rosa moyesii "Geranium"

Rosa moyesii "Geranium"

The species is a beautiful shrub with blood-red single flowers about 2-3 inches across, followed by large, crimson, flagon-shaped hips. But it is a large and rather gaunt shrub, so the more compact variety "Geranium" is a better choice for a small garden. Even so it needs a lot of space to grow to its full potential. Although it is a smaller plant, the flowers and hips are just as spectacular as the species, and perhaps even more so.

Size	Height: 8 ft. Spread: 7 ft.
Flowering	Mid summer
Uses	Border
Scent	No scent

77

Old Garden Roses

T owards the end of the eighteenth century, intrepid plant collectors returned from the Far East with roses that carried the most coveted of genes: the ability to flower more than once each year. These first imports were crossed with their European cousins to produce the direct parents of the modern rose. The early novelties of the 1800s, along with their ancestors, make up that intriguing section in rose catalogs called "The old garden roses", a title recently updated to "heritage roses". Heritage roses are exclusively shrubs that in the main have rather a lax habit and vary in height from 2 to 6 feet. These old roses are easy to grow. Their constitution is very strong – indeed they would not be in existence today if it were otherwise – and at the same time, they retain their novelty value. Another interesting feature is that many of the older varieties can produce exciting variations, such as

Right: *Rosa gallica* "Charles de Mills" is a beautiful old rose with an exciting petal formation. This vigorous plant can grow to about 5 feet tall.

Large, dark green leaves support the purple-red flowers in midsummer.

The large double blooms of *Rosa Rugosa* "Blanc Double de Coubert" are purest white and heavily scented. The plant has tough, leathery leaves and grows to about 5 feet. Like most rugosas, it will make a good hedge.

The weight of the blooms produces swathes of tumbling flowers.

Once the blooms are past their best, deadhead them heavily to encourage strong, new growth.

"Rosa Mundi", "Baron Girod de l'Ain" and "Mme. Pierre Oger". The history and development of the rose is a living spectacle that has given rise to an industry devoted to immortalizing these lovely flowers, whether it be reproducing them for decorative purposes or preserving the real thing.

Rosa gallica officinalis

The Apothecary's Rose is steeped in history, and many people grow it for that reason. It is the ancestor of many of today's red hybrid tea and floribunda roses. The large, semi-double, light crimson flowers open wide to show the central bold stamens, and are followed later by small, round, red hips. Unfortunately this is one of those roses particularly prone to blackspot so be prepared to spray if this disease is a problem in your area.

Size	Height: 4 ft. Spread: 3 ft.
Flowering	Early and mid summer
Uses	Borders
Scent	Strong fragrance

Rosa gallica officinalis

Rosa gallica "Versicolor"

Rosa gallica "Versicolor"

Rosa Mundi, as it is also known, has been a favorite with rose-lovers for hundreds of years. The distinctive crimson and white striped flowers are always eye-catching, which, coupled with this variety's long history, gives it a special place among shrub roses. You need only one in a border to make a bold splash of color with its bizarre and beautiful blooms. There are problems, however, and you will have to keep an eye open for mildew, especially in the fall.

Size	Height: 4 ft. Spread: 4 ft.
Flowering	Early and mid summer
Uses	Borders
Scent	Strong fragrance

A Selection of Old Garden Roses

Baron Girod de l'Ain
Blanc Double de Coubert*
Cécile Brunner
Charles de Mills*
Common Moss (Pink)*
Comte de Chambord*
Fantin-Latour*
Ferdinand Pichard
Great Maiden's Blush*
Louise Odier*
Mme. Hardy*
Mme. Isaac Perreire*
Mme. Pierre Oger*
Paul Neyron*
Rosa Mundi (*R. Gallica* "Versicolor")*
Roseraie de l'Hay*
Souvenir du Dr Jamain*
Variegata di Bologna*
William Lobb (Old Velvet Moss)
Zéphirine Drouhin*

* Fragrant flowers

Left: Lovely *Rosa bourboniana* "Louise Odier" has large incurved double blooms of rose-pink shaded lilac, with a pleasant fragrance. The plant has an arching habit and grows to 4 feet.

Above: *Rosa gallica* "Versicolor" ("Rosa Mundi") is probably the oldest heritage rose commonly grown today. In early summer, masses of striped blooms appear on a relatively short plant about 3 feet tall.

The gallicas flower only once, but the blooms last for a long time and can be used to create stunning floral art decorations.

Penelope

This tried and trusted Hybrid Musk rose is one of the best. The large trusses of shell pink, lemon-centered flowers are produced in abundance, and they fill the air with a strong musk rose fragrance. The flowers are bright pinky-orange in bud but change to softer shades as they open. Coral pink hips follow as a bonus. The plant is very free-flowering, has a compact and neat growth habit, and is set off by attractive dark foliage. It makes a superb rose hedge.

Size	Height: 3 ft. Spread: 4 ft.
Flowering	Early summer
Uses	Borders, hedge
Scent	Strong fragrance

Left and below: Penelope

Petite de Hollande

Petite de Hollande

A classic among the Centifolia roses, it has been known since the end of the 18th century. The exquisitely formed, small Centifolia type flowers are pink, deepening towards the edges. They are almost pompon-like, as the variety's alternative name "Pompon des Dames" suggests. The flowers are very fragrant and freely produced on arching stems. The small size of the flowers does not detract from its value as a decorative rose in the garden.

Size	Height: 4 ft. Spread: 3 ft.
Flowering	Early and mid summer
Uses	Borders
Scent	Strong fragrance

Hybrid Tea Bush Roses

The legendary hybrid tea rose has classically-shaped blooms, is easy to grow and the most recent introductions are very tough and relatively disease-free. All hybrid teas produce large blooms throughout the summer. The first hybrid teas were inevitably limited in color range, but in this century breeders have successfully introduced the most vivid yellows, startling vermilions, a host of blends and bicolors, blues and now grays, greens and stripes. Many famous examples are household names. "Peace" – appropriately named in 1946 after World War Two – is famous for its wondrous growth and perfection of bloom, "Tropicana" ("Super Star") is an extraordinary vermilion, and the more recent "Silver Jubilee" is a subtle blend of pinks and boasts a high flower rate. The majority of hybrid teas are cultivated in individual rose beds, either singly or in groups of color or variety. To encourage them to give of their best, make sure you prepare the soil well, prune them every year in spring and give them an occasional feed. All are hardy and thrive in normal temperate climates. Like all types of rose they will benefit from full sunlight, but semi-shade is not impossible.

"Blessings" could well be described as the perfect hybrid tea rose. It is a beautiful coral salmon color, with fragrant blooms and an even growth that will fill a bed and provide abundant flower throughout the summer and fall. The even, deep green foliage is very hardy and disease-resistant, a perfect foil for the bloom.

This bloom will look good for another three or four days.

Once the color begins to fade, deadhead the rose, removing old blooms to allow new branches to develop.

For decorative purposes, cut the rose at this stage and enjoy its beauty as it opens.

Left: Although "Peace" is an old rose by modern standards, it remains very popular and deserves its reputation as the most famous rose ever bred. It will make a large shrub if lightly pruned.

7

Nevada

Even gardeners who are not passionate about shrub roses usually know and like "Nevada". It belongs to the Modern Shrub group and is one of the most popular of all shrub roses. The whole bush is covered with large, semi-double, creamy-white flowers about 4 inches across in early summer. The only problems are its vulnerability to blackspot and a tall, arching habit that gobbles up space. Although it will flower spasmodically later, it is really a rose of early summer.

Size	Height: 7 ft. Spread: 7 ft.
Flowering	Early summer
Uses	Borders
Scent	Reasonably fragrant

Nevada

Paulii Rosea

Paulii Rosea

This a real charmer, closely resembling a wild rose in color and appearance: a single flower with half-folded, bright pink petals, white at the base. The problem is finding a suitable spot to grow it. This hybrid between *R. rugosa* and *R. arvensis* makes a huge mound of shoots, forming a prickly thicket. Grow it as a ground cover over a bank, or to cover an unsightly tree stump. It can also be treated as a climber if planted against a wall.

Size	Height: 5 ft. Spread: 15 ft.
Flowering	Early and mid summer
Uses	See above
Scent	Strong fragrance

A Selection of Fragrant Hybrid Tea Roses

Alec's Red
Blessings
Fragrant Cloud
Fragrant House
Keepsake
Loving Memory
Heart Throb (Paul Shirville)
Fragrant Charm 84 (Royal William)
Solitaire
Troika

A Selection of Large-flowered Hybrid Tea Roses

Freedom
Ingrid Bergman
Just Joey
Loving Memory
Pascali
Peace
Savoy Hotel
Silver Jubilee
Rock-n-Roll (Tango)
Tequila Sunrise

"Just Joey's" coppery orange blooms have a unique coloring. Acclaimed as a breakthrough on account of its novel petal formation, this rose has earned many awards. It flowers early and will grow in the most uncompromising soils. An application of fertilizer in midsummer encourages beautiful fall color.

Left: Large-flowered roses, such as "Heart Throb" ("Paul Shirville") shown here, are just as attractive when all the blooms are full out. The peach-shaded, salmon pink flowers on a plant of medium height have a delightful fragrance.

Above: "Tequila Sunrise" is one of the most exciting new roses recently introduced. The spectacular deep yellow blooms are heavily edged in vivid scarlet and retain their color for a long time.

Mrs. Anthony Waterer

A Rugosa hybrid, "Mrs. Anthony Waterer" dates back to the last century. If you can put up with a short flowering season, its prolific show of semi-double crimson blooms in early summer will not disappoint. It may produce a few more flowers towards the fall, but seldom enough to make a show. As with most old roses, you can depend on a strong scent. The shrub tends to grow rather large for most modern gardens, but looks good in a rose or mixed border.

Size	Height: 5 ft. Spread: 5 ft.
Flowering	Early summer
Uses	Borders
Scent	Strong fragrance

Mrs. Anthony Waterer

Madame Hardy

Madame Hardy

D amask roses are elegant shrubs with nicely cut foliage, and "Madame Hardy" brings the cool appearance of white. It has been around for a long time – over 160 years – but still finds a place in the rose catalogs. It is a truly beautiful rose, with fairly large cup-shaped blooms with a green eye, set against abundant foliage. It has an upright growth habit. This is one of the traditional old roses that it is difficult to omit in a collection of such types.

Size	Height: 5 ft. Spread: 4 ft.
Flowering	Early and mid summer
Uses	Borders
Scent	Strong fragrance

Floribunda Bush Roses

By definition, a floribunda bush rose is any variety that bears clusters or sprays of flowers. Because of its checkered history and development, this group has been known by several names, including *hybrid polyanthas,* Poulsen roses and grandifloras. Although "cluster-flowered" is the newest and probably most accurate description, the most commonly accepted term remains floribunda. Essentially, hybrid teas and floribundas are both bush roses requiring identical care. Where they do differ is in their flower potential. A hybrid tea is a large bloom borne singly on a stem, whereas a floribunda is a cluster of blooms, no single flower being dominant or larger than any other. There is the added bonus that a cluster provides a longer flowering period. Take care when selecting floribundas as they can vary tremendously in height.

Take care when positioning roses of this color; pinks can clash violently.

"Memento" dies prettily, which is a bonus when large heads are difficult to deadhead.

Above: Because of its continuity, "Memento" has been compared with "Iceberg". The large clusters of salmon-vermilion, medium-sized flowers are a feast of color all summer, growing on an average-sized bush about 3 feet tall with strong healthy foliage.

"Margaret Merrill" has exceptionally large flowers for a floribunda rose, white with a hint of blush. The very sweetly scented plants are of medium height, with deep green, large, leathery foliage. An ideal variety that fills a bed to perfection.

Although there is some variation in hybrid teas, the differences are not so obvious, but certain varieties of floribunda can grow as much as 36 inches taller than others. At one time, floribundas were said to be tougher than hybrid teas, but today all roses are more resilient. Like hybrid teas, floribundas are ideal for formal beds, although they will grow virtually anywhere, provided they are maintained properly. When grown in groups they can lend color to a dull shrub border and their color range is equal to any other type of rose. To ensure a continuity of flower, be sure to deadhead immediately after the first flush of flower. A midsummer feed is essential.

L. D. Braithwaite

The New English roses are becoming popular with shrub rose enthusiasts, combining the appearance of the true old-fashioned roses with the longer flowering period of modern varieties. "L. D. Braithwaite" is one of the best of them for continuity of bloom, which it combines with top quality flowers and a good scent. The full-petaled blooms are brilliant crimson, rather cup-shaped when fully open, and have the strong fragrance typical of old roses.

Size	Height: 4 ft. Spread: 4 ft.
Flowering	Early to late summer
Uses	Borders
Scent	Strong fragrance

L. D. Braithwaite

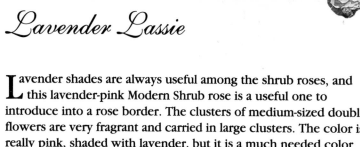

Lavender Lassie

Lavender Lassie

Lavender shades are always useful among the shrub roses, and this lavender-pink Modern Shrub rose is a useful one to introduce into a rose border. The clusters of medium-sized double flowers are very fragrant and carried in large clusters. The color is really pink, shaded with lavender, but it is a much needed color among this group of roses. Because "Lavender Lassie" is repeat flowering you can depend on color spread throughout the summer.

Size	Height: 4 ft. Spread: 3 ft.
Flowering	Early to late summer
Uses	Borders
Scent	Strong fragrance

A Selection of Floribunda Bush Roses

Amber Queen*
Dicky (Anisley Dickson)
Anna Livia
Arthur Bell*
English Miss*
Fragrant Delight*
Hannah Gordon
Harvest Fayre*
Iceberg
Sunsprite (Korresia)*

Margaret Merrill*
Memento
Scented Air*
Shocking Blue*
Southampton*
The Times Rose
Trumpeter

* Fragrant Flowers

Left: "Arthur Bell" is a good, strong, yellow rose that will do well at the back of a border or in the middle of a bed to give height. The well-shaped blooms with a sweet scent are produced in small clusters on a vigorous bush with deep green, healthy foliage. It is one of the first to flower, but needs vigorous deadheading.

The secret of a good floribunda is the constant renewal of young growth.

"English Miss" is a pretty blush that blends well in color schemes without clashing with some of the more strident colors. The plant is of medium height, with handsome mid-green foliage and flowers early in the season with a pleasing fragrance.

10

John Hopper

This old Hybrid Perpetual was raised over 130 years ago, but you can still find it if you go to some of the nurseries specializing in old-fashioned roses. The double pink flowers have an almost ruffled look, but like many of these older roses the color fades dramatically as the blooms age, becoming mauve. It makes quite a large, thorny bush, so needs careful positioning. It often looks best in a border devoted to old-fashioned shrub roses.

Size	Height: 5 ft. Spread: 4 ft.
Flowering	Early to late summer
Uses	Borders
Scent	Strong fragrance

Kathryn Morley

Kathryn Morley

This New English rose has cup-shaped, clear pink flowers coupled with a very appealing fragrance. The flowers have a dainty appearance but the plant is robust and free-flowering, blooming with abundance over a long period. Its compact size – much smaller than most shrub roses – makes it particularly suitable for a small garden. The variety was was named by auction – the right to name it raising $19,500 for a charity.

Size	Height: 2½ ft. Spread: 2 ft.
Flowering	Early to late summer
Uses	Beds, borders
Scent	Strong fragrance

John Hopper

Modern Shrub Roses

What is a modern shrub rose? Strictly speaking, all roses are shrubs, but the modern conventional hybrid tea or floribunda has come to be accepted as a bush, while the more prolific and bigger plant is designated a shrub. For practical purposes, we could say that a modern shrub is a floribunda trimmed to shape and not cut down hard every spring. Although many people assume that a modern rose is by definition repeat flowering, this is not necessarily true of all the varieties in this group. The majority produce magnificent splashes of color in high summer, followed by a small flush in the fall. They respond well to extra rose fertilizer applied as soon as the summer flush has finished to goad them into another display in fall. They also benefit from heavy deadheading.

"Ballerina" is a prolific shrub that grows to 4 feet tall and wide. Its seemingly continuous sprays of bloom are reminiscent of phlox.

Modern shrub roses play a most important part in the design of mixed flowering shrub borders, providing color when most other flowering plants have finished for the season. Very few varieties will make a splash when planted singly; the finest effects are achieved by planting them in threes or fives. Whatever the plan, make sure that the plants have plenty of light, particularly in the spring. Do not be tempted to plant early flowering bulbs at the base of shrub roses, as this impedes the roses' cultivation and feeding.

"Frühlingsgold" is one of a small family of modern shrubs with the prefix "Frühling", meaning spring. These vigorous plants appear to thrive on neglect. The large, pale yellow, single blooms have a wild rose scent.

Jenny Duval

This Gallica rose of unknown origin was first recorded in 1821, and the flower form shows its age. It nevertheless has a charm and fragrance that appeals to lovers of old roses. The attractive buds open into bright flowers that are a blend of purple and violet, though red is the dominant first impression. The blooms fade to pale lilac at the edges. The exact color depends largely on environmental factors such as temperature.

Size	Height: 4 ft. Spread: 3 ft.
Flowering	Early and mid summer
Uses	Borders
Scent	Strong fragrance

Jenny Duval

Jacques Cartier

Jacques Cartier

This Portland rose variety is now over 120 years old, but is still grown as an example of the relevance of these traditional types in today's garden. Its large, flat-looking flowers are a rich pink, matched by an equally strong fragrance. Although it flowers for most of the summer, it is rather less "perpetual" than some similar varieties. Like other Portland roses it grows into a compact shrub with the flowers held close to the foliage.

Size	Height: 4 ft. Spread: 3 ft.
Flowering	Early to late summer
Uses	Beds, borders
Scent	Strong fragrance

A Selection of Modern Shrub Roses

Ballerina
Buff Beauty*
Cerise Bouquet
Felicia*
Frühlingsgold*
Golden Wings
Graham Thomas*
Kordes' Robusta
Lichtkönigen Lucia
Nevada

* Fragrant Flowers

"English Roses" vary in height and garden worthiness, but make adaptable shrubs.

Always allow "Graham Thomas" to grow naturally. Do not stake the plant unless it is absolutely necessary – the result is unattractive to look at.

Left: "Graham Thomas" is a truly magnificent yellow shrub rose with an appealing scent. It is the best – and certainly the healthiest – of the new "English Roses", and can be expected to attain a height of 4 feet.

Above: No other shrub rose can grow to 8-10 feet high and wide and flower as profusely as this "Marguerite Hilling". It requires no pruning and produces a modest second crop of large, single, flushed pink flowers in fall. It has an equally spectacular creamy white sister, "Nevada".

Shrub roses respond to heavy deadheading immediately after the first flush of flower to encourage bloom in the fall.

Henri Martin

Moss roses are a mutation of *Rosa centifolia,* having developed a moss-like growth around the buds and flowers. They are not grown much now but were once very popular, and "Henri Martin" has been around for about 130 years. The long buds are covered with a light green "moss", opening to reveal crimson, semi-double blooms. These are held in graceful clusters, and the plant makes an attractive feature in a mixed border.

Size	Height: 5 ft. Spread: 4 ft.
Flowering	Early and mid summer
Uses	Borders
Scent	Some scent

Henri Martin

Jacqueline du Pré

Jacqueline du Pré

This tough, modern shrub rose is easy to grow, and is likely to flourish even in less than ideal conditions. The semi-double white flowers open to reveal prominent stamens, and look rather like a white Christmas rose *(Helleborus niger)*. It blooms freely all summer and will often carry on even into fall, filling the air with a delightful musk scent. Where conditions suit it may grow larger than suggested below, so give it plenty of space.

Size	Height: 6 ft. Spread: 4 ft.
Flowering	Early to late summer
Uses	Borders
Scent	Strong fragrance

69

Climbers and Ramblers

Until 1800, cultivated roses were a mixture of shrubs and bushes and it was not until new plant forms were introduced from the Far East that it was possible to grow roses to equal the vigor of climbers in other families of flowering plants. The rapid expansion of climbing roses produced a vast range of varieties, many still familiar today. The old ramblers, such as "Dorothy Perkins", "Paul's Scarlet" and "American Pillar", vied for popularity with the climbers – "Spanish Beauty" ("Mme. Grégoire Staechelin"), "Mme. Alfred Carrière" and "Climbing Mrs Sam McGredy" – all of which leads to the question, 'What is the difference between a climber and a rambler?' The short answer is that a rambler has pliable stems and is happier on a fence or trellis that will provide ample support, whereas the wood of a climber is stouter and more suitable for a wall, which offers less support. At one time, with one or two exceptions, ramblers and climbers only flowered once a year, but modern varieties can produce as much bloom in the fall as in high summer. Today, climbers and ramblers are cataloged as summer-flowering, recurrent-flowering, etc, but most modern recurrent flowering climbers do not have the same vigor as their ancestors.

"Sympathie" is a vigorous plant with deep bronze foliage and scarlet crimson flowers during summer and fall.

Above: "Bantry Bay" is an ideal climber for the small garden. Good quality blooms flourish on a plant that is easy to control, growing to about 10 feet.

13

Graham Thomas

This is one of the finest New English roses, named after one of the most influential enthusiasts of old roses. The very full, cup-shaped golden double flowers have a strong tea rose fragrance, and the abundant light green foliage makes a good backdrop for them. This is a very beautiful and desirable rose, and compact enough to include in most gardens. It successfully combines the charm of the old-fashioned roses with the longer flowering period of modern roses.

Size	Height: 4 ft. Spread: 4 ft.
Flowering	Early to late summer
Uses	Beds, borders
Scent	Strong fragrance

Graham Thomas

Henri Foucquier

Henri Foucquier

Not among the most popular of the Gallica shrub roses, you may have to search for a supplier, but it is nevertheless a pretty rose. It makes a lax bush with almost thornless stems and matt, mid-green leaves that go well with the pink of the rather loose double flowers. The blooms are very large and circular, composed of many petals that reflex once open and fade to mauve-pink. Henri Foucquier (1838-1901) was a French writer and politician.

Size	Height: 3 ft. Spread: 3 ft.
Flowering	Mid summer
Uses	Borders
Scent	Some scent

Pillar Roses

Aloha*
Bantry Bay
Dublin Bay
Golden Showers*
Handel
Laura Ford
Warm Welcome
White Cockade

Walls

Climbing Iceberg
Dreaming Spires*
Guinea
Mme. Alfred Carrière*
Maigold*
Mermaid
Parade
Summer Wine*

Into Trees

Albertine*
Bobbie James
Cécile Brunner (climbing)
Paul's Scarlet*
Rosa filipes "Kiftsgate'*
The Garland
Wedding Day

North and East-facing Aspects

Spectacular (Danse de Feu)
Dortmund
Gloire de Dijon*
Maigold*
Mermaid
Mme. Alfred Carrière*
The New Dawn*
Zéphirine Drouhin*

Fences

Compassion*
Spectacular (Danse de Feu)
Dortmund
Félicité et Perpétue

Grand Hotel
Malaga*
Sympathie

Right: *Rosa filipes* "Kiftsgate" can grow through trees to 15 feet. The creamy scented flowers are followed by many small, round, bright red hips.

Left: Select appropriate varieties with care. "Golden Showers" is almost perpetually in bloom, but do not expect it to climb through trees.

Fu Dagmar Hastrup

"Frau Dagmar Hastrup" and "Frau Dagmar Hartopp" are among the variations sometimes used for this important Rugosa variety. It is considered by many experts to be the best of the Rugosas, and excellent as a rose hedge. It flowers over a long period, has good scent, and shows disease resistance. The clear, pale pink single flowers are very beautiful, and finally there are the splendid hips to round off the display in fall.

Size	Height: 4 ft. Spread: 4 ft.
Flowering	Early to late summer
Uses	Borders, hedge
Scent	Reasonably fragrant

Left and below:
Fu Dagmar Hastrup

Gertrude Jekyll

Gertrude Jekyll

This is a New English rose with large, rosette-shaped flowers. The color is rich, glowing pink, the fragrance powerful and the blooms long-lasting. Although the growth is rather lanky, the variety combines a traditional old-fashioned look and strong scent with a long flowering period. The mid green foliage shows good disease resistance, making this a trouble-free plant for a shrub border. It is also compact enough to grow in a rose bed if you prefer.

Size	Height: 4 ft. Spread: 2½ ft.
Flowering	Early to late summer
Uses	Beds, borders
Scent	Strong fragrance

Standard Roses

The standard or tree rose became very popular about 100 years ago. Until then, roses were either grown on their own roots (from cuttings) or from seed. Once it was discovered that a superior product could be produced from propagating on a rootstock, it was a short step to producing plants on an elongated stem, however artificial they looked. After a decline in popularity, standard roses are back in fashion, the quality of stock has improved and gardeners like the height they can add to an otherwise flat-looking rose bed. Choose standard varieties with care; not every bush rose will make a good standard, which should be vigorous but bushy. Many of the newer shrub roses and even ground cover varieties produce admirable heads. Take care when positioning standard roses, as they cannot tolerate windy conditions. In any case, always stake the plants securely. If you are using a standard to add height to a rose bed, consider the vigor of the bedding variety growing beneath the standard. Some bedding roses grow too tall and will overwhelm a good standard.

With careful deadheading, this beautiful pink and ivory variety will contribute to the beauty of your garden for a long period during the summer and fall.

Right: "Hannah Gordon" is a popular floribunda that will also excel as a standard. Its pleasing distribution of foliage and flower is an asset in any garden. With light pruning, it will eventually grow into a massive plant.

Left: "Peer Gynt" is a good yellow rose with an iron constitution that will produce high-quality blooms. As the petals age, they assume a bright red flush. A well-grown head carries large clusters of perfectly shaped flowers.

15

Fantin-Latour

A classic among shrub roses, "Fantin-Latour" is usually considered to be a Rosa centifolia hybrid, but there is speculation about the influence of other rose types in its history. It has the "cabbage rose" influence, with cup-shaped blooms, though with age the outer petals reflex. The color is a charming pale pink deepening to shell pink in the center. The fragrance is delicate rather than strong, but it is still an outstanding variety.

Size	Height: 6 ft. Spread: 5 ft.
Flowering	Mid summer
Uses	Border, cutting
Scent	Reasonably fragrant

Fantin Latour

Ferdinand Pichard

Ferdinand Pichard

Hybrid Perpetuals were at their peak a hundred years ago, but dropped in popularity because they are rather too tall for most small, modern gardens. If you have the space, however, try "Ferdinand Pichard", a bushy plant with pink flowers heavily streaked and splashed with crimson. It is the sort of coloring that seldom fails to attract attention and comment. Its continuous flowering and rich fragrance combined with unusual markings make this a desirable rose.

Size	Height: 5 ft. Spread: 4 ft.
Flowering	Early to late summer
Uses	Borders
Scent	Strong fragrance

A Selection of Standard Roses

Hybrid tea and floribunda

Anna Livia
Blessings
Iceberg
Keepsake
Loving Memory
Peace
Silver Jubilee
Trumpeter

Shrub

Ballerina
Canary Bird
Kent
Nozomi
Snow Carpet
Surrey
The Fairy

Weeping

Albéric Barbier
Crimson Shower
Dorothy Perkins
François Juranville

Right: "Nozomi" is one of many ground cover roses that will produce the most beautiful heads. This spectacular standard requires little or no pruning, yet will develop in a very pleasing manner, with swathes of blooms about 36 inches long.

Left: "Iceberg" is probably the most recurrent-flowering floribunda and will amply repay a good feeding program. With light pruning it will develop a very large standard head.

Below: "Félicité et Perpétue", a classic example of a rambler budded onto a stem, makes a very good weeping standard. Cut out old flowering wood, but allow the plant to grow naturally.

Evelyn

This is a recent addition to the New English roses, and is bound to delight rose lovers. Like most of the New English roses, this one is repeat flowering and will bloom on and off for most of the summer. The large flowers are full of petals, forming a shallow cup. The coloring is deep apricot, sometimes with a hint of yellow. Fragrance is also a feature. It makes a compact shrub, compact enough for small gardens as well as large ones.

Size	Height: 4 ft. Spread: 3 ft.
Flowering	Early to late summer
Uses	Borders
Scent	Strong scent

Evelyn

Duchess de Montebello

Duchess de Montebello

A Gallica-Damask hybrid, this vigorous and spreading bush has fully double, pure blush-pink blooms, set amid light green foliage. The effect is one of delicate charm and cottage garden atmosphere. The fragrance is good too. Details of its origin are not known for certain, but it was bred prior to 1929, when it was first recorded. The lax growth makes it a difficult shrub to place in a small garden, but it is easy to accommodate in a large shrub border.

Size	Height: 5 ft. Spread: 4 ft.
Flowering	Mid summer
Uses	Borders
Scent	Strong fragrance

65

Patio and Miniature Roses

Until recently, rose producers and gardeners accepted that the typical modern rose should be a statuesque plant topped off with the perfect bloom. However, since many rose varieties are simply not suitable for the small garden, the idea emerged of designing a low-growing rose that retained the flower form of the modern bush but was suitable for a small patio or yard. The result was the patio rose, an easy to control, short-growing floribunda bearing conventionally shaped, but tiny blooms. Even smaller than the patio rose, the true miniature rose is happier in a pot or grown as a forcing variety for the pot rose market. Both patio and miniature roses will thrive in the modern garden. However, just because they are small, do not be tempted to plant them in rockeries or on alpine slopes, where they will surely die. They are true roses and require the same cultivation as any of the larger varieties.

Left: "Baby Masquerade" grows about 12 inches high. The flowers turn from yellow to red as they age. Deadhead for flowers in fall.

Above: "The Queen Mother Rose" is an ideal plant for the small garden. The beautifully rounded plants, about 18 inches high, will produce a feast of pure soft pink flowers with a pleasing fragrance. They continue from midsummer until fall.

This reliable, healthy plant flowers a little later than most patio roses. If lightly pruned, it develops into a small shrub.

17

Constance Spry

Charles de Mills

A modern shrub rose, it is sometimes classed as a New English rose (a group of plants bred from "old-fashioned" roses but with the influence of modern breeding – including a long flowering period). This one unfortunately has only a brief flowering period, but it is one of the most sought-after and is now widely available. The clear pink blooms are exceptionally large, with a very sweet fragrance. The growth is lax and it can be grown against a wall as a climber.

Size	Height: 7 ft. Spread: 7 ft.
Flowering	Early summer
Uses	Borders, against a wall
Scent	Strong fragrance

Constance Spry

Charles de Mills

This strong-growing Gallica rose has outstandingly fragrant, bold and distinctive flowers that make it one of the best of its group. The color is crimson but fades to reddish-purple with age; the whole flower has a rather flat and "sliced off" appearance that make the petals look very tightly packed. This beautiful old rose is vigorous and undemanding to grow yet remains compact enough for even a modest shrub border.

Size	Height: 5 ft. Spread: 4 ft.
Flowering	Mid summer
Uses	Borders
Scent	Exceptional fragrance

A Selection of Patio Roses

Anna Ford
Gentle Touch
Little Bo Peep
Brass Ring (Peek a Boo)
Perestroika
The Queen Mother Rose
Buffalo Bill/Young Mistress (Regensberg)
St Boniface
Sweet Dream
Sweet Magic

Remember to repot miniature roses every year. For best results, grow the plants in clay pots, where the roots are much happier and remain cooler. The plants will also be healthier and produce more flower.

Above: "Little Artist" is a complete novelty among the miniature roses. The scarlet blooms with a white eye are exciting to grow. They are easily grown from cuttings and will flower throughout the summer.

Right: "Sweet Sunblaze" ("Pretty Polly") could be described as a designer rose made for the pot. This reliable patio rose has clear pink blooms about 2 inches across that produce a veritable blaze of color.

18

Cerise Bouquet

One of the best of the larger modern shrub roses, "Cerise Bouquet" grows into a big, robust shrub with arching growth. Although the cerise-pink, semi-double flowers are not large, they look spectacular carried in big, open sprays on long stalks. Many people think the fragrance has distinct raspberry overtones. Unfortunately the growth is too tall and vigorous for a small garden, but it looks good as a background plant for a large mixed border.

Size	Height: 9 ft. Spread: 8 ft.
Flowering	Mid and late summer
Uses	Borders
Scent	Strong scent

Cerise Bouquet

Celestina

Celestina

This old Damask rose was introduced prior to 1750, and having been cultivated for so long deserves a place in any collection of shrub roses. The large, semi-double flowers are carried in small clusters, creating a graceful effect against the gray-green foliage. The color is blush pink, with the golden stamens adding to the fresh effect. Do not regard this rose simply as an historic variety from the past, it is a beautiful and worthwhile shrub to have in your garden.

Size	Height: 5 ft. Spread: 4 ft.
Flowering	Early and mid summer
Uses	Borders
Scent	Reasonably fragrant

Ground Cover Roses

In response to the demand for roses to provide color on difficult slopes, road verges, grassy banks and in other informal planting schemes, breeders have developed prostrate or semi-prostrate plants that need little or no maintenance, no pruning, and that provide a lengthy flowering period and great resistance to disease. At first, the color range was limited to pinks and whites, followed by good reds, while the yellow varieties were large, sprawling plants that flowered once, but patient development has resulted in recurrent flowering ground cover roses in a full color range, compact enough even for the smallest garden. Take care to choose the correct variety for a specific location, however, and be sure to differentiate between the sometimes enormous varieties, such as "Red Max Graf" or "Pheasant", and the more restrained growth of "Suffolk" and "Snow Carpet". Ground cover roses appreciate as much light as possible and like to have their roots in fertile soil. They will grow in semi-shade, but do not expect so much flower. They will provide cover and color in most hostile situations, as well as helping to keep weeds at bay.

Never prune this type of rose. Allow it to grow naturally and accumulate a "cushion" of foliage.

Most modern ground cover roses will grow from cuttings. They require only the minimum of pruning.

Right: *Rosa* "Bonica" is a popular environmental plant, widely grown in the USA. Sprays of pastel pink, small double blooms are produced form midsummer until fall and cover banks and "green" areas.

Below: The "County" series of ground cover roses provide color and green foliage in many difficult situations. "Essex" is ideal for the small garden and flowers all through the summer.

"Essex" has small, pretty pink flowers and disease-resistant foliage.

19

Buff Beauty

Classed as a Hybrid Musk rose, "Buff Beauty" has big flowers in a color that one associates more with modern roses (the variety was introduced in 1939). The buff-yellow blooms, which fade to a warm ivory, are borne in large clusters. Although the flowers are very shapely in bud, they become loose when they are fully open. The foliage is particularly handsome and luxuriant, but susceptibility to mildew is another drawback.

Size	Height: 5 ft. Spread: 5 ft.
Flowering	Early to late summer
Uses	Borders
Scent	Strong fragrance

Buff Beauty

Céleste

Céleste

You will sometimes find this Alba rose sold as "Celestial". It makes a large, rounded bush with big, sweetly-scented semi-double shell-pink flowers. The cupped blooms sit upright on a tidy-looking plant, and look especially good against the gray-green foliage. The variety originated in Holland around the end of the 18th century. The Alba roses tolerate shade better than most, and "Céleste" is really tough and undemanding despite the delicate charm of its blooms.

Size	Height: 6 ft. Spread: 4 ft.
Flowering	Mid summer
Uses	Borders, hedge
Scent	Strong fragrance

A Selection of Ground Cover Roses

For the big garden

Ferdy
Grouse
Pheasant
Pink Bells
Red Max Graf
White Bells
White Max Graf

For the small garden

Flower Carpet
Kent
Northamptonshire
Nozomi
Snow Carpet
Suffolk
Surrey
The Fairy

Left: "Grouse" is the first of the new generation of ground cover roses. It is capable of growing 8-10 feet in a season. In midsummer it is covered with heavily scented, small, very pale pink flowers.

Above: "Suffolk" will cover an average area of 11 square feet. It will grow little taller than 12 inches. Clusters of bright scarlet flowers persist from midsummer to late fall.

Alain Blanchard

This Gallica rose was raised more than 150 years ago. The semi-double, almost single, flowers open purple-crimson, but sometimes look purple mottled crimson as the blooms age. They are almost cup-shaped, with a mass of attractive golden stamens. The thin, wiry growth starts to tumble forwards once it reaches about 4 ft, so do not plant it too near the front of the border. The fragrance is as good as you would expect from these old-fashioned roses.

Size	Height: 4 ft. Spread: 3 ft.
Flowering	Early and mid summer
Uses	Borders
Scent	Strong fragrance

Alain Blanchard

Belle Isis

Belle Isis

Try this pretty Gallica rose if you have a small garden and are unable to accommodate the larger varieties. The rather floppy growth usually restricts itself to about 3 feet, with a similar spread. The flowers are a delicate flesh-pink, refreshingly different from the reds of most Gallicas. It has been suggested that it might be a hybrid with a Centifolia rose, but its pedigree is less important that the charm of its full-petaled flowers.

Size	Height: 3 ft. Spread: 3 ft.
Flowering	Early and mid summer
Uses	Borders
Scent	Strong fragrance

Choosing & Planting Roses

Shrub Roses

Choosing A Good Plant

A rose tree takes two years to produce. It must be lifted, graded, stored and is eventually despatched as a bare root plant between fall and spring. Alternatively, it is root-wrapped for sale off the shelf or containerized (potted) for sale in spring or summer. Problems can arise during this process, but a top-quality plant is easy to recognize.

If the roots look brown and old, the plant has probably been potted too long.

Shoots are very tender at this stage and easily damaged, which will retard progress by some weeks.

You can always identify an old plant by the color of the wood. A fresh and healthy plant is a bright, deep green.

Bad Plant

Sometimes the stock onto which the rose is budded produces extraneous growths called suckers, which should have been removed.

Good Plant

In a good plant there should be a minimum of three strong roots and a root system free of snags and breakages.

The wrapping keeps the plant moist. Do not allow it to dry out after purchase.

Bad Plant

This is typical of the poorest type of containerized rose plant. It was probably potted on too late and offered for sale the following spring.

Good Plant

By its very nature, a rose bush is not the ideal subject for containerization. Given a good-quality compost, the roots will grow very quickly and soon fill out the pot. Look for good, strong growth and make sure that the foliage is free of disease and the plant is well watered.

Bad Plant

This plant has been on the shelf too long and is beginning to make growth.

Good Plant

This is a well cared-for plant. Cut the tie after planting.

Scintillation

Unlike the prostrate ground cover roses represented by the County series (see "Hertfordshire"), this is really a shrub rose that you can train as a ground cover by pegging down the sprawling stems. You can also let it grow over the stumps of old trees, clamber over a bank, or simply grow it as a sprawling, free-standing shrub. It produces a mass of semi-double, blush-pink flowers in large clusters, filling the air with fragrance.

Size	Height: 4 ft. (less if pegged down)
Flowering	Early summer
Uses	Ground cover
Scent	Strong fragrance

Scintillation

Zéphirine Drouhin

Zéphirine Drouhin

A star among climbers, this carmine pink, semi-double thornless climbing Bourbon has been popular for more than 120 years. Despite its age, you will find it stocked by most rose growers, and extolled wherever it is planted. You can grow it as a hedge or tall bush by suitable training and pruning, but it is usually grown as a climber. Deadhead regularly to keep it flowering well throughout the summer. The main drawback is a susceptibility to mildew.

Size	Height: 10 ft.
Flowering	Early to late summer
Uses	Walls, fences
Scent	Strong fragrance

Choosing The Best Location

Roses appreciate a location in full sunlight and out of cold drafts. However, semi-shade is often acceptable, particularly for the new ground cover varieties. Roses need water, so avoid planting them in a dry position, such as a rockery. Remember that standard roses need adequate staking and are not really suitable for very open, windy positions. Make sure that all roses receive the maximum amount of light in spring and do not allow heavy-leaved plants, such as tulips, to grow too close to the base of the bushes. Also, avoid smothering the base with dense creeping ground cover plants.

Above: Carefully mark out the planting positions of the roses. The general rule is to allow 24 inches between bushes for beautiful, well-grown plants with plenty of space.

Right: Here the vigorous rambler "Albertine", the slow-growing climber "Pink Perpétue" and the shrub rose "Ballerina" complement each other superbly.

Below: The hybrid tea "Rosemary Harkness" is typical of the many roses that will thrive almost anywhere, but whose flower potential is determined by the amount of light they receive.

Roses planted on the shady side of the bed are clearly at a disadvantage.

Here, the roses benefit dramatically from full sun.

Rosa filipes "Kiftsgate"

If you want to include a famous climber that everyone will know, this is a good candidate, but you need a large garden in which to grow it. Given the chance it will grow to about 30 feet, ideal for growing though old trees or scrambling along a hedge, but too vigorous for a small garden. The small, single, creamy-white flowers are very fragrant and produced in profusion. The numerous small red hips in fall bring a touch of late color to the garden.

Size	Height: 30 ft.
Flowering	Early summer
Uses	Through trees, along hedges, covering outbuildings
Scent	Good fragrance

Rosa filipes "Kiftsgate"

Sander's White

Sander's White

Perhaps the best small, semi-double white rambler, the flowers are well set off by dark, glossy foliage. It was raised over 80 years ago and has stood the test of time. Its exceptional fragrance has helped it keep a place in the catalogs of specialist growers. It only flowers once, but later than most ramblers, so it helps to spread the period of interest if planted as a companion to brighter ramblers that flower early. A nice rambler for a wall.

Size	Height: 10 ft.
Flowering	Mid summer
Uses	Walls, fences, pergolas
Scent	Exceptional fragrance

Making The Best of Your Soil

The rose is a very tolerant plant that will thrive in most soils. However, it does have some essential requirements and the first of these is good drainage, which means that surplus water in the soil should drain away efficiently. Winter flooding does not appear to be detrimental, but continuously wet conditions are not good. Soils can vary from the lightest sand to the heaviest clay and from alkaline, chalky soils to acidic, peaty ones. Chalky soils are not particularly good for growing roses, but you can improve them by adding peat or peat substitute and feeding the plants with a foliar feed, but this can be expensive. Sandy soils are easier to handle, but are sometimes described as "hungry" because they absorb organic material very quickly. The remedy is to build up the food availability with copious amounts of well-rotted compost or farmyard manure. Heavy soils have a reputation for producing the best roses, but this is largely a fallacy. They need breaking up with organic material and sand to avoid becoming waterlogged. The ideal soil for cultivating roses is a well-drained, deep loam. Do remember that you cannot successfully replant an old rose bed with new roses until the bed has had a rest period – usually for about three years. Alternatively, replace all the old soil.

There are several test kits you can use to register the acidity or alkalinity of your soil. The ideal pH level is 6.5, which is slightly acid.

Follow the instructions carefully, collecting the soil you wish to test from about 9 inches below the surface.

Chopped bark is a suitable top dressing and subdues weeds. Remember to give the plants a feed, as there is no food value in raw bark.

Good-quality sharp sand helps to break up heavy clay soil, aids drainage and makes it easier for the fibrous roots to take up food.

Adding ground limestone is the most appropriate way to correct a very acid soil. Spreading about 2 ounces per square yard every two years will give good results.

Pink Bells

This is typical of the ground cover roses that have an arching, ground-hugging habit rather than the prostrate growth represented by "Hertfordshire". The arching shoots spread wide but create a mound about 2½ feet high. The shoots are well clothed with small, dark green leaves, and the large clusters of quite small, soft pink flowers nestle among them. Be prepared to peg the shoots down for a couple of years to create spreading, even cover.

Size	Height: 2½ ft. Spread: 4 ft.
Flowering	Early to late summer
Uses	Ground cover
Scent	No scent

Pink Bells

Paul's Himalayan Musk

Paul's Himalayan Musk

This is one to choose if you want a vigorous climber that will cover most things, and it is a good rose for a very large pergola. It is one of the best for planting to scramble into a tree. The long, trailing growth will spread horizontally if it is unable to grow upwards, so this in not one to plant where space is restricted. The dainty, creamy blush-pink semi-double flowers, with a hint of soft lilac, hang down in large fragrant sprays.

Size	Height: 30 ft.
Flowering	Early summer
Uses	Pergolas (large), through trees
Scent	Strong fragrance

Planting A Bush Rose

You can plant a bush rose in two forms – bare-rooted or containerized. In either case, prepare the ground by digging over the soil and incorporating well-rotted garden compost or farmyard manure into the top layer. In many soils, this is only possible when the earth is very dry; never handle soil when it is waterlogged. If possible, break up the sub-soil below the cultivated top layer. Use a suitable planting mixture around the roots. For the best results, plant bare-rooted roses in the fall. If the plants are dry, soak them in a bucket of water for about two hours and then plant them out straightaway.

1 Prepare a hole 12 inches across and deep, with a stick in the corner. Place the plant against the stick, allowing a free run of the roots.

2 The junction of the root system and the wood of the tree should be at surface level. Add a good spadeful of planting mixture to cover the roots.

3 Fill the rest of the hole with soil, making sure that any manure added in the course of preparing the site does not touch the plant's roots.

4 Ideally, firm in the soil thoroughly around the roots. If conditions are unfavorable, wait until the soil is dry or in a more friable state.

Madame Alfred Carrière

This is one of the few Noisette climbers still grown, yet they used to be used widely to clothe cottage gardens and castles. This one has survived because it is still one of the best roses for a shady wall. The large, fragrant blooms appear steadily for most of the summer, and even into fall. The cupped flowers are white tinted flesh pink. Although over 100 years old, this disease-resistant and vigorous climber is still well worth growing.

Size	Height: 20 ft.
Flowering	Early to late summer
Uses	Walls
Scent	Strong fragrance

Madame Alfred Carrière

New Dawn

New Dawn

This forerunner of the modern perpetual-flowering climbers, popular for over 60 years, is still one of the best. The semi-double, shell pink flowers are relatively small but produced in great numbers. The flexible growth is ideal for training over an arch or pergola, but it will do well on pillars and fences and on walls. To add to its versatility, it makes a pretty cut flower. You can even grow it as a large, free-standing shrub. Repeat flowering performance is also good.

Size	Height: 10 ft.
Flowering	Early to late summer
Uses	Walls, fences, arches and pergolas, pillars, cutting
Scent	Reasonably fragrant

57

Planting A Containerized Bush Rose

Although containerized plants are available all year round, the best time to plant them is in late spring or early summer. The very nature of the root system of a containerized rose does not lend itself to mishandling, so avoid disturbing the root ball when taking the plant out of the container.

1 Today, most roses are containerized in a rigid pot, which makes extracting them simple. A good sharp tap will allow the plant to drop out without root damage.

Avoid damaging this well-developed network of fine feeding roots.

2 Place the plant in the prepared hole approximately 12 inches across and deep. Add a spadeful of planting mixture around the roots. Avoid damage to roots or foliage.

3 Fill in the hole with a planting mixture. Either buy this from a garden shop or prepare it by mixing a handful of bonemeal in a large bucket of moist peat or peat substitute.

4 Make sure the plant is securely anchored. Be sure to water it with about a gallon of water and maintain this level of watering on a weekly basis until it is well established.

Helen Knight

You might find this listed in some catalogs as *Rosa ecae* "Helen Knight", in others simply under its varietal name. The flowers are larger than on the species itself, and it is altogether a better garden plant, covering a wall with deep yellow single flowers in early summer. It arose as a chance seedling at the Director's house at the Royal Horticultural Society's garden in England. *Rosa pimpinellifolia* "Grandiflora", which was growing nearby, could be the other parent.

Size	Height: 10 ft.
Flowering	Early summer
Uses	Walls
Scent	No scent

Helen Knight

Hertforshire

Hertfordshire

Some traditional shrub roses are recommended for ground-cover if they have a prostrate or ground-smothering growth habit, but the County series of ground cover roses is quite distinct. These varieties are not only ground-hugging but repeat-flowering too, blooming all summer and even into fall. "Hertfordshire" is just one of a whole series named after different English counties. This one has a profusion of carmine-pink single flowers.

Size	Height: 1 ft. Spread: 3 ft.
Flowering	Early to late summer
Uses	Ground cover
Scent	No scent

Planting Climbers and Ramblers

Establishing the correct planting position and selecting the appropriate variety is of paramount importance when planting climbers and ramblers. If the rose is to grow against a wall or in a restricted space, a moderate climber is ideal. Against a fence you will require something a little more vigorous, while a trellis will accommodate most types of climber or rambler. Prepare the plant support and build posts or trellis in position before planting the rose.

"Handel" is a stunning climber that grows to about 10 feet and is ideal for the smaller garden.

1 Prepare a planting hole measuring about 12 inches across and deep. If available, work a forkful of well-rotted compost into the soil below the plant, but not touching the roots.

2 Position the rose. Add a bucket of planting mixture around the roots. Use peat or peat substitute, mixed with a handful of bonemeal or a ready-made mixture. Fill the hole with soil.

3 New climbers and ramblers have normally been trimmed down to 24 inches before delivery. Cut the restraining string. Make sure the soil around the roots is well firmed in.

4 Although a newly planted climber or rambler may appear to be short, tie it into its support immediately, carefully spreading out the branches and securing them with soft string.

Handel

Goldfinch

"Handel" is quite exceptional. Its main claim to fame is its lovely coloring, unusual among climbers. The blooms have a good hybrid tea shape, but the distinctive coloring is its main attraction: creamy-blush rimmed rosy-red. This stunning color combination really is eye-catching. The flowers are also good enough to show, and they make an attractive cut flower. Drawbacks are poor fragrance and susceptibility to blackspot and mildew.

Size	Height: 10 ft.
Flowering	Early to late summer
Uses	Walls, pillars, cutting, exhibition
Scent	Some scent

Handel

Goldfinch

This is not a rose that will shout at you across the garden, but one to plant for scent and subtle enjoyment. The small flowers open yellow but fade to white in the sun, creating a blend of yellow, cream and white. It only blooms once, but when it does the flowers are produced in large clusters, backed by pale green leaves. This very hardy and vigorous rambler grows quite large, and looks especially effective when growing through a tree.

Size	Height: 10 ft.
Flowering	Early summer
Uses	Walls, through trees
Scent	Strong fragrance

Planting A Standard Rose

Choose a position that offers the best protection from the wind and stake the rose securely so that it quickly becomes established and grows on strongly. Never allow the plant's roots to dry out. As a precaution, heel the roses in as soon as you bring them back from the nursery. To do this, dig a shallow trench and lay the plant at an angle of 45° so that the roots are in the trench. Cover the roots with loose soil to keep the plant in good condition. If necessary, dip the roots in water first. In any case, they will certainly benefit from being dipped just before they are planted. This does not mean watering them once they are in the ground, although this might be helpful in a very dry season.

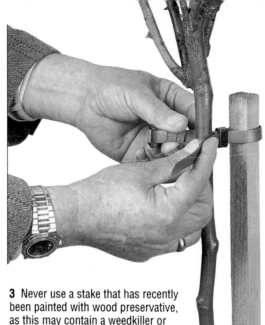

"Memento"

1 Drive a firm stake made of straight-grained, knot-free wood into the hole. Put the stake on the side facing the prevailing wind. Because the roots of a standard are larger than those of a bush rose, make the planting hole correspondingly larger. Spread roots out evenly in the hole.

2 Offer up the rose to ensure it is in the right position. Make sure the junction of the root and stem is level with the top of the soil. If planted any deeper, growth will be stunted and if planted any shallower, the roots are at risk from drying out.

3 Never use a stake that has recently been painted with wood preservative, as this may contain a weedkiller or other chemicals that harm plants.

When firmly anchored, the top of the stake should reach to just below the first shoot.

Use a good quality strap to secure the rose to the stake. Never use plastic twine, which is abrasive and can cause considerable damage to the stem.

Adjust the tie as the stem thickens.

4 Cover the roots entirely with a good planting mixture or mix your own, using one bucket of peat or peat substitute to a handful of bonemeal.

5 Tread the soil in firmly around the roots to help them become established. This may not be possible in wet weather, but is essential before the tree starts to grow in the spring.

Dublin Bay

This is one to go for if you want a large-flowered red climber for a pillar. The brilliant blood red, medium-sized flowers are large and beautifully formed, and the plant is exceptionally free-flowering. Plenty of leaves prevent the plant looking bare after flowering. The main flush of flowers is in early summer, with intermittent blooms afterwards, and often a respectable second show in the fall. Best for fences and pillars.

Size	Height: 15 ft.
Flowering	Early to late summer
Uses	Pillars, fences
Scent	Some scent

Dublin Bay

Francis E. Lester

Francis E. Lester

This rambling Hybrid Musk will grow tall up a wall. It can be trained to a more modest height up a post or along a wall, but is at its best when allowed plenty of space. It is a robust plant, smothered in single white flowers, pink in bud, that fill the air with fragrance. Small, orange-red hips in fall extend the interest. Although not the most popular rambler, perhaps because it needs plenty of space, it will bring real charm and a lovely fragrance to your garden.

Size	Height: 15 ft.
Flowering	Early and mid summer
Uses	Walls, pillars, fences
Scent	Exceptional fragrance

Pests and Diseases

To produce healthy plants, rose growers rely principally on a program of proper feeding and protection from insects and diseases. This means applying a good rose fertilizer at the appropriate time, but never a food that is high in nitrogen, unless you want big blooms for showing. Keep dead wood to a minimum and remove it in early fall, when it is much easier to identify. The most common rose diseases are caused by fungi that find a haven in the plant. Sometimes they are simply unsightly, as in mildew, but black spot and rust cause leaf fall, which is harmful to plants. Spray affected roses with the appropriate product, carefully following the manufacturer's instructions. Pests are very easy to deal with; a good spray in early summer will discourage most of them. Identify the culprit, spray and systematically clean all utensils after use. In some places, rabbits and deer can become a nuisance. Although there are several remedies to discourage them, in the long term adequate fencing is the only solution. Occasionally a rose becomes weak or appears not to thrive and is always the first to succumb to disease. If this happens, remove the plant rather than embark on expensive remedies. Unfortunately there is nothing you can do to anticipate this problem.

Left: Unsightly galls, such as this spiked pea gall, are caused by wasps. Control these by using insecticides.

Gather up and burn the diseased, fallen yellow leaves. Remove old and decaying wood that harbors dormant spores.

Above: These lackey moth caterpillars create bivouacs of spun thread and devour large quantities of rose leaves. Spray caterpillars with a specially formulated insecticide.

Below: Leaf-cutter bees, seasonal, short-lived predators, can cause this damage. Control by spraying.

Right: Aphids, or greenfly, suck the sap on young rose shoots, but are easily controlled with modern systemic sprays or organically-produced natural products.

Left: Black spot is a common and damaging fungal disease that will eventually result in the loss of infected leaves. Some varieties appear very prone to this disease and are being phased out.

Crimson Shower

There are brighter and more prolific ramblers, but this is an excellent one to add if you already have a few of the more fragrant and brighter varieties. It will follow on where the others leave off, producing its large clusters of rosette-shaped crimson blooms when the other ramblers have passed their best. It blooms prolifically and late, and by planting it next to an early-flowering variety you can extend the period of interest. Good disease resistance is a bonus.

Size	Height: 15 ft.
Flowering	Mid and late summer
Uses	Walls, pillars, pergolas and arches
Scent	Some scent

Crimson Shower

Dortmund

Dortmund

An outstanding climber apart from the lack of scent, and versatile, too. It is excellent grown up a pillar, but can be used as a large shrub instead if you prune it appropriately. The large, single flowers are bright red with a white eye, punctuated by yellow stamens. Blooming is continuous throughout the summer if you remove the dead flowers regularly. The abundant foliage is glossy and a good backdrop for the dazzling flowers.

Size	Height: 8 ft.
Flowering	Early to late summer
Uses	Walls, pillars
Scent	No scent

Above: Leaf-rolling sawflies produce this effect when they lay eggs in the leaves. Kill larvae by spraying soil in spring.

Right: The white coating is caused by mildew, a fungal disease encouraged by high humidity. Some varieties are very prone to mildew; control it with regular spraying.

Below: Grubs and Japanese beetles have a voracious appetite for roses. Simply pick them off by hand.

Above: Viruses have little effect on healthy roses. Good feeding is a help. Keep tools clean to avoid contamination.

Above: Leaves infected with rust, a fungus, eventually turn yellow and drop off. Deter with a specialized fungicide.

Bantry Bay

Not everyone wants a rampant rambler, and if you need one with restrained growth, perhaps to grow up a pillar, "Bantry Bay" is a good choice. The shapely buds open to semi-double pale rose pink blooms in large, well-spaced trusses. And unlike many ramblers it is repeat flowering, so you will have some flowers later in the summer after the first flush. It lacks a strong scent, but is worth seeking out for its pretty blooms and good disease resistance.

Size	Height: 10 ft.
Flowering	Early and late summer
Uses	Pillars, fences
Scent	Some scent

Bantry Bay

Climbing Cécile Brunner

The ordinary "Cécile Brunner" is a miniature hybrid tea that grows to about 2½ feet, but the climbing version can easily grow to 15 feet, so it is important to be careful about the word "climbing" when ordering! The clusters of pale pink flowers, borne along the shoots, are rather loose and lack a good shape, but stand out well against the dark foliage. There are a few flowers later in the season, but only the early summer flush is impressive.

Size	Height: 15 ft.
Flowering	Early and mid summer
Uses	Walls, through trees
Scent	Some scent

Winter Protection

Modern rose plants are hardy specimens that can withstand a considerable degree of frost. The secret of producing strong plants lies in feeding your plants at the right time. Early in spring, apply good quality, well-prepared compost to raise the fertility of the soil. To harden roses to make them strong enough to face the cold, apply extra potash in early summer. In areas that experience very windy weather, cut down rose bushes to 24 inches after the first frosts so that their top growth will not rock in the wind and thus loosen the plant in the soil. You could also try covering them if you wish. Never handle plants in a frozen condition and do not prune them until the ground has totally thawed out.

1 The commonest method of protection against frost damage is to "shroud" the entire plant with a dry material, such as shredded bark.

Place three or four canes around the plant to support garden netting or fine mesh chicken wire.

1 In hard conditions you may need to cover the plant completely. Reduce the bush to about 12 inches in height and loosely fill a large container, such as a pot, with straw.

2 Gently place the pot over the rose. If using an old plastic bucket, you will need to stabilize it with a heavy weight.

2 Fill the enclosed container with the dry material. In spring, remove the netting and prune the plant as usual. Disperse the insulating material around the bed as a mulch.

Wrapping the head of a standard rose in straw protects it against the ravages of winter.

Albertine

For many people this is the rambler against which others are measured, although it is not without problems. The vigorous branching growth is covered with pale pink double blooms and coppery buds, all strikingly set off by dark green foliage. The sweetly fragrant flowers are unfortunately easily damaged by heavy rain. Mildew is another problem. Despite these drawbacks this is a rambler that is sure to attract admiration.

Size	Height: 20 ft.
Flowering	Early summer
Uses	Walls, arches and pergolas
Scent	Strong fragrance

Albertine

American Pillar

American Pillar

A rampant rambler with white-eyed, single, bright pink flowers. It has been popular since it was introduced at the beginning of the century, and because of its vigorous growth is often planted so that it can scramble into a tree. It needs a lot of pruning for a more restrained position. Although still a popular variety, there are others just as attractive with fewer drawbacks, which include susceptibility to mildew and growth that is difficult to control where space is limited.

Size	Height: 20 ft.
Flowering	Mid summer
Uses	Pergolas, through trees
Scent	No scent

Pruning Roses

Ramblers & Climbers

Basic Pruning Techniques

The average rose is a very tough individual that will withstand a tremendous amount of abuse and neglect, but also responds well to some very elementary management. By the very nature of its breeding, a modern rose plant needs to be controlled if it is to provide a fine display in the garden. Pruning simply means reducing the plant seasonally so that it makes new growth and bears superior bloom. In the early spring, the process is called pruning, in the summer, deadheading, and in the fall, cutting back to face the winter. It is vital to prevent a rose expending its energy on maintaining old wood that has fulfilled its function and that will only harbor disease. A golden rule is never to cut a rose plant when the wood is in a frozen state or during a hot, dry spell. And remember that species roses and the majority of old garden roses do not require the same harsh treatment as the sophisticated modern hybrids.

Where to make the cut

This cut has been made too close to the bud. Once the bud has grown, it will blow out in the wind due to lack of adequate support.

In this example, the length of wood left on the branch above the bud is far too long. The stem will "die back" and harbor disease spores.

A jagged cut means that your pruning shears are not sharp. Damaged wood will create a haven for small insects and other creatures.

This is the ideal length to aim for when pruning. The slanted cut will soon heal and the bud will develop into a strong branch.

Pruning a maiden bush

A young rose bush newly planted in the fall will need pruning in the spring of its first year. Cut the plant back to about 5 inches above the ground. It is likely that the soil around the rose will have been loosened by winter frosts, so it is a good idea to firm it down again in the spring when you prune the rose back. Remember that newly planted roses do not need feeding during their first growing season.

Yesterday

This rose can seem a bit of a mystery to anyone trying to find it. You will quite rightly find it listed with the floribundas in many catalogs, but those with a "patio rose" section will probably place it there. Others list it as a shrub rose. It is worth the search because it smells good and looks good. Sprays of lilac-pink to rosy-violet flower are carried in fragrant clusters on long, spreading shoots. Try it simply as a shrub in the border, and cut some sprays for the house.

Size	Height: 3 ft. Spread: 3 ft.
Flowering	Early to late summer
Uses	Borders, cutting
Scent	Reasonably fragrant

Yesterday

The Times Rose

The Times Rose

A bed of "The Times Rose" is a real eye-catcher with its profusion of large clusters of crimson-scarlet flowers. The double, rosette-like flowers almost seem to glow when the sun catches the petals, and they last well indoors. This variety, which is listed in some catalogs simply as "The Times", makes a bushy plant, with plentiful, deep green, glossy foliage that is tinted bronze-red when young. Disease resistance is good.

Size	Height: 2½ ft. Spread: 2 ft.
Flowering	Early to late summer
Uses	Beds, cutting
Scent	Some scent

50

Pruning Equipment

Sharp long arms or "parrot bills", as shown bottom right, are ideal for the task of removing old branches. Fall is the best season to do this, as dead wood is much easier to identify at this time.

You will need a strong implement to remove larger stems. The pruning saw being used on the right will remove the largest branches and very good designs are now available. If you can get close to the base of the plant, hold the stem as you saw through it.

Most branches can be cut back with a pair of sharp pruning shears, but never attempt to cut back dead wood with these, as it will ruin the cutting edge with very costly consequences.

Side-by-side pruning shears produce a clean cut, are easy to maintain and stay sharp.

Strong gloves are essential. Thorns can cause nasty injuries.

Sheila's Perfume

This is a rose with many merits. The good-sized blooms shade from yellow in the center to pinkish-red at the edge, and have a strong scent for a floribunda. They grow on strong, straight stems, making it a good cut flower (it looks good and smells good in a vase or flower arrangement), but do not have the vibrancy of color to make an outstanding general garden display. This superb rose is best appreciated at close quarters.

Size	Height: 3 ft. Spread: 2 ft.
Flowering	Early to late summer
Uses	Beds, cutting, exhibition
Scent	Strong fragrance

Sheila's Perfume

Tango

Tango

"Tango" packs a real punch and manages to create a sense of vibrant movement. The flat, semi-double flowers combine a happy blending of orange-red and pale yellow, the paler colors giving each bloom a bright "eye". Flowering is prolific, and the bushy plants make it a good choice for mass planting in a bed. The mid green glossy foliage has good disease resistance. If the scent were stronger this would be a tip-top bedding rose.

Size	Height: 3 ft. Spread: 2 ft.
Flowering	Early to late summer
Uses	Beds, exhibition
Scent	Some scent

Pruning A Wild or Species Rose

By definition, a wild rose is a species that has existed for hundreds of years and flourished without any outside help. In the wild, aging branches occasionally die back and subsequently rot away. In the garden, you can assist this process by completely removing the offending branches. Most wild roses will grow in a garden environment without any form of control. By their nature, the majority flower only once in the season, followed by hips in the fall. Therefore, there are two golden rules: never shorten good, well-grown stems, since the branches must be allowed to grow naturally, and never deadhead or you will not get hips in the fall. Many wild roses can grow tall and straggly, usually in an effort to reach the light, and become quite ugly and a general nuisance. There is a simple but drastic remedy for this problem that rarely fails. In late fall or early winter, saw the whole plant down to about 12 inches from the ground. This can also be done as soon as flowering has finished. The result is a proliferation of young wood. The first growth after this treatment may not yield flower, but this is a small price to pay for a dramatic improvement to both the plant and garden.

Rosa gallica "Complicata" will make a big rambling shrub not unlike an enormous blackberry bush. The beautiful large, single, pink flowers with golden centers smother the plant in midsummer.

33

Princess Alice

This has won more than half a dozen international awards, and has special qualities among the yellow floribundas. The color is bright without any pronounced shading, and the hybrid-tea-shaped flowers are particularly well formed. The blooms are well spaced on very large trusses, almost like a natural bouquet, and it makes a particularly good cut flower. It grows rather tall for bedding in a small garden, but is very suitable for exhibition.

Size Height: 3-4 ft. Spread: 2-2½ ft.
Flowering Early to late summer
Uses Beds, borders, cutting, exhibition
Scent Some scent

Princess Alice

Princess Michael of Kent

Princess Michael of Kent

Another first-rate yellow floribunda, more compact than "Princess Alice" and therefore more suitable for a small garden. The canary yellow flowers are large, well shaped, and freely produced. They contrast well against the shiny green foliage. Reasonable fragrance is a bonus, as is the good disease resistance. This is a variety that scores very highly on both the quality of the individual flowers and on the overall garden impact.

Size Height: 2-2½ ft.
Spread: 2 ft.
Flowering Early to late summer
Uses Beds
Scent Reasonably fragrant

2 Occasionally an unsightly scar is left where a branch has been cut out. You can paint this with grafting wax or a suitable dressing obtainable from good gardening shops. Do not be tempted to use a wood preservative. If the scar is torn, clean it up first with a sharp knife.

3 Cutting back old branches is an easy operation but take care that, having sawn off the branch, you pull it out of the tree without causing any damage. If you should accidentally damage the top branches of the bush, trim them with a pair of sharp pruning shears to neaten them up.

A good saw is essential for pruning wild roses. Wear your oldest clothes and be sure to put on thick gardening gloves.

Do not attempt to prune these plants in the spring.

1 A wild rose will take kindly to the occasional removal of one or two old branches. These are easy to identify, as they turn brown with age. This work is best done in early winter.

Stones may lodge in the lower branches of old trees. Remove them to avoid damage to the saw.

Picasso

A once great rose, "Picasso" was the first of its type, red with a white center and irregular splashes of white or pink. As with many roses, the actual color varies in shade and intensity depending on how long the flower has been open, and on the time of year. In the 20-plus years that this variety has been around there have been improvements and newer varieties that look similar generally perform better and are less prone to blackspot.

Size	Height: 2½ ft. Spread: 2 ft.
Flowering	Early to late summer
Uses	Beds
Scent	No scent

Picasso

Mounbatten

Mountbatten

An outstanding rose with bold trusses of mimosa yellow, hybrid-tea-shaped blooms, and a reasonable fragrance. It has been used in royal wedding bouquets, so it can be taken as an acceptable cut flower. The buds open into double flowers with petals that first reflex and then incurve, creating an interesting and changing shape. The abundant leaves generally clothe the plant all over, and have a high disease resistance. It may be too tall for a very small garden.

Size	Height: 3-4 ft. Spread: 2½ ft.
Flowering	Early to late summer
Uses	Beds, borders, cutting, hedge, exhibition
Scent	Reasonably fragrant

47

Pruning A Bush Rose

Both hybrid tea and floribunda bush roses are recurrent-flowering, which means that every branch has the potential to produce bloom. However, once the stem has fulfilled its function, it must either be removed or at least cut back. Most plants naturally accumulate a tremendous amount of small spindly wood, old parts of the plant die back and strong shoots need controlling. In the summer, this process is called deadheading, but in spring the treatment is more severe and is described as pruning. For the plant to realize its full potential, it is vital to remove the non-productive branches every spring, otherwise they will impede the performance of the plant during the following flowering season. In bush roses, this means cutting out considerable quantities of old wood. Pruning also helps to keep plants healthy, as weak shoots are natural habitats for overwintering diseases, and a plant needs a

Ideally, cut this type of wood back in the fall.

This flowering wood developed in the fall and has been killed by frost.

Never cut back to thin wood, as it cannot produce strong growth.

Some of this top growth will have young green buds that must be removed. The are premature and probably frost-damaged.

Cut the branch on the slant. It will heal more easily and a slanted cut will not harbor moisture that encourages disease.

1 This plant has survived the winter. If it is a newly planted or replanted specimen, it may need firming into the ground before being pruned.

2 Remove some older branches completely, using a pair of long-handled pruners. Never use your best pruning shears to cut out dead wood.

strong base if it is to support good, strong shoots. Prune bush roses in the spring, In the fall, it is a good idea to cut the plant back by about a third overall. Reducing the height helps the plant to avoid wind damage and loosening of the roots in winter gales – the cause of more fatalities than hard weather.

3 The most important function of pruning is to remove the old, spindly growth, which will only harbor disease if left on the plant and reduce the quality of flower.

Memento

If you live in an area where the summers are usually wet and you like red floribunda roses, then "Memento" should please. Its flat, salmon-vermilion, medium-sized flowers are very rain-tolerant and produced in large clusters with great gusto over a long period. The dense mid-green glossy foliage is also produced in profusion, with a respectable degree of disease resistance. This is a good rose for a massed display in a difficult season.

Size	Height: 2½ ft. Spread: 2 ft.
Flowering	Early to late summer
Uses	Bedding
Scent	Some scent

Memento

Molly McGredy

Molly McGredy

Bi-colors are not to everyone's taste, but many find that they have a special appeal. If you like bi-colors and floribundas with hybrid-tea-shaped bloom, then "Molly McGredy" is sure to be an attraction. Now over 20 years old, the variety has lost some of its earlier appeal, but it remains free-flowering in the garden, and still looks attractive on the show bench. Disease resistance is good, but you will be disappointed if you expect fragrance too.

Size	Height: 2½ ft. Spread: 2 ft.
Flowering	Early to late summer
Uses	Beds, exhibition
Scent	No scent

46

4 Having removed old and diseased branches, reduce the remaining wood by two-thirds, the average proportion for most varieties.

5 Cut back the branch to an outside eye – a dormant bud growing outwards. Buds growing towards the center produce an unattractive bush.

"Iceberg", a fine free-flowering bush rose, can be conventionally pruned or trimmed as a shrub. Trim off small branches that could harbor disease. An exceptional rose that will grow anywhere.

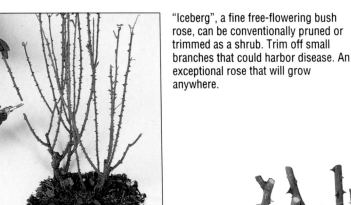

6 Resist the temptation to "light" prune – bush roses are never damaged by hard pruning. Cut out all damaged branches.

7 As the pruning proceeds and the bush reveals itself, look it over to make sure you have not missed a dead branch.

8 The final result is a neat, clean-looking plant devoid of all rubbish. Leave a good framework of strong wood to produce a later harvest of blooms.

Len Turner

L en Turner was the Secretary of The Royal National Rose Society between 1965 and 1983, so you can be sure that a rose chosen to bear his name is a good one. The creamy white flowers, edged pink, are carried on compact bushes with plenty of healthy-looking, mid-green foliage. The blooms have a fairly loose, open appearance, and they lack a strong scent – but this is a rose you will simply want to grow for its delightful color combination.

Size	Height: 1½-2ft.
	Spread 1½ ft.
Flowering	Early to late summer
Uses	Beds
Scent	Some scent

Len Turner

Matangi

Matangi

T his is one of those vibrant-looking floribundas that creates a bright splash of orange-vermilion from a distance. Closer inspection will reveal a silver shading at the base of the petal and on the reverse. The flowers are produced in great profusion, and it is an excellent rose for bedding. As well as attractive flowers it has glossy, healthy-looking foliage that has good disease resistance. The flowers also stand up well to wet weather.

Size	Height: 2½ ft. Spread: 2½ ft.
Flowering	Early to late summer
Uses	Beds
Scent	Some scent

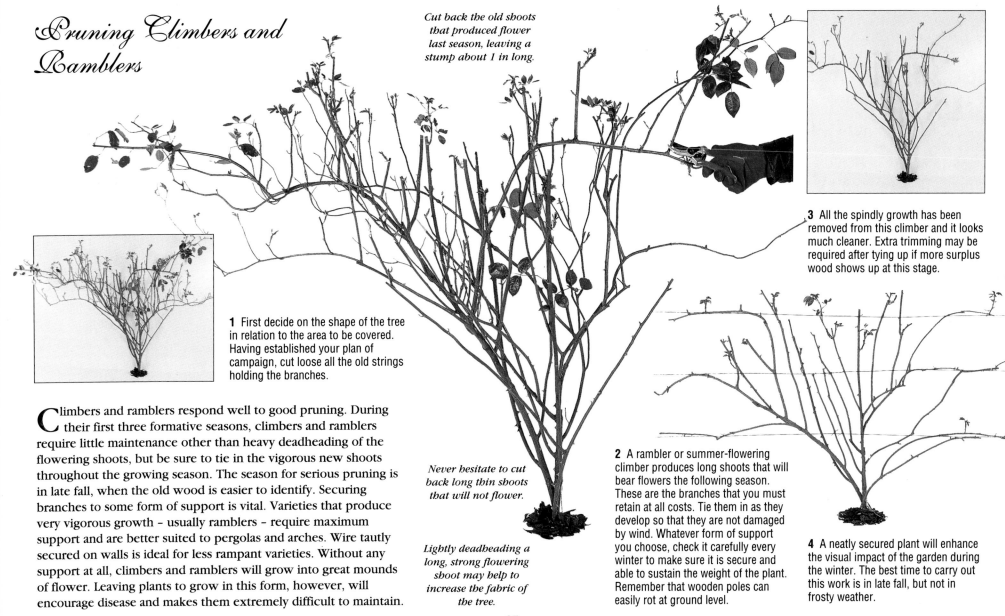

Pruning Climbers and Ramblers

Cut back the old shoots that produced flower last season, leaving a stump about 1 in long.

3 All the spindly growth has been removed from this climber and it looks much cleaner. Extra trimming may be required after tying up if more surplus wood shows up at this stage.

1 First decide on the shape of the tree in relation to the area to be covered. Having established your plan of campaign, cut loose all the old strings holding the branches.

Climbers and ramblers respond well to good pruning. During their first three formative seasons, climbers and ramblers require little maintenance other than heavy deadheading of the flowering shoots, but be sure to tie in the vigorous new shoots throughout the growing season. The season for serious pruning is in late fall, when the old wood is easier to identify. Securing branches to some form of support is vital. Varieties that produce very vigorous growth – usually ramblers – require maximum support and are better suited to pergolas and arches. Wire tautly secured on walls is ideal for less rampant varieties. Without any support at all, climbers and ramblers will grow into great mounds of flower. Leaving plants to grow in this form, however, will encourage disease and makes them extremely difficult to maintain.

Never hesitate to cut back long thin shoots that will not flower.

Lightly deadheading a long, strong flowering shoot may help to increase the fabric of the tree.

2 A rambler or summer-flowering climber produces long shoots that will bear flowers the following season. These are the branches that you must retain at all costs. Tie them in as they develop so that they are not damaged by wind. Whatever form of support you choose, check it carefully every winter to make sure it is secure and able to sustain the weight of the plant. Remember that wooden poles can easily rot at ground level.

4 A neatly secured plant will enhance the visual impact of the garden during the winter. The best time to carry out this work is in late fall, but not in frosty weather.

Intrigue

The name suggests something dark and mysterious, and the color is deep and intense. The deep crimson, semi-double blooms have the appearance of velvet, but open to show contrasting golden stamens. This is one of the darkest floribundas you will find, and a good choice if you love dark red roses. For general garden display, however, it can appear rather dull. The trusses and flowers are large and good enough to show.

Size Height: 2½ ft. Spread: 2 ft.
Flowering Early to late summer
Uses Beds, exhibition
Scent Some scent

Intrigue

Korresia

Korresia

An excellent yellow floribunda with a long track record of reliable performance. The color is clear and bright and does not easily fade. Fully double flowers and a good fragrance are other desirable features. The flowers really stand out and are borne on a bushy plant with dark green, glossy foliage. Disease resistance is good. This is a first rate floribunda for bedding and has to be towards the top of the shopping list for yellows.

Size Height: 2½ ft. Spread: 2 ft.
Flowering Early to late summer
Uses Beds, exhibition
Scent Strong fragrance

44

"Albertine" flowers briefly in midsummer. Tie in the ensuing growth so that it blooms the following year.

Tying a climbing rose

The art of persuading a climbing plant to produce the maximum amount of flower is to create stress on the branches. This is done quite simply by bending them over in an arched fashion. A vertical stem will only flower at the end of the branch. The result of tying branches horizontally is that they not only produce more bloom, but will cover a greater area and new shoots are encouraged to grow from the base.

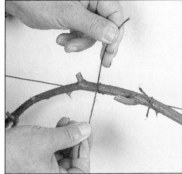

Always use soft natural string, never plastic-coated wire.

Cut the ties with a sharp knife.

International Herald Tribune

A rose for the modern, small garden, this dwarf floribunda is often described as a patio rose because it makes a dwarf, bushy plant compact enough to be grown in a pot and will look in proportion in a small bed on the patio. This outstanding variety has won top rose awards in several countries, and it is one to choose if you want a really disease-resistant variety. The color is a distinctive violet, bordering on lilac-purple.

Size	Height: 1½-2 ft. Spread: 1½ ft.
Flowering	Early to late summer
Uses	Beds, patio, pots
Scent	Some scent

International Herald Tribune

Iceberg

Iceberg

After more than 30 years you will still find this in almost every rose catalog, which is testimony to its outstanding qualities. The white flowers, tinged pink in bud, are produced in profusion in large clusters. This beauty is matched by a tough constitution: the variety is well known for its toughness, vigor and longevity. It looks right almost anywhere, including shrub and mixed borders, as well as in beds, but remember that it needs lots of space.

Size	Height: 3-5 ft. Spread: 3-4 ft.
Flowering	Early to late summer
Uses	Beds, borders, hedge
Scent	Some scent

Pruning A Standard Rose

"Sweet Magic", a patio standard, grows to about 18 inches high, with beautifully formed orange and gold fragrant blooms in perfect proportion to the healthy medium-green foliage.

A standard rose is a bush rose that has been propagated like any other rose, but onto a stem that gives it height. Similarly, a shrub standard is a shrub on a stem and a weeper is a rambler on a tall stem. The same pruning principles apply to a standard variety as to the normal form, but bearing in mind the eventual shape of a standard in full flower, you may decide to keep a branch that you would have cut from a bush. Standards need a firm stake and the correct size of strap to support them. Remove the strap regularly and test the strength of the stake; you may even find that the plant is supporting the stake! Replace the strap as the stem thickens. Remember that the stem of a standard is some form of wild rose and may produce suckers. If you spot these early in the growing season, you can rub them off. Later in the year, you will need pruning shears to remove them. If a standard is growing with bush roses, prune the bush roses first so you can reach the standard rose more easily.

1 This magnificent head will require considerable thinning. The aim is to cut out all the ugly shoots and aging wood. Before starting to prune, check the state of the stake and tie. They become brittle and quickly rot away.

2 The first step is to thin out the plant, removing all the twiggy growth. This includes the occasional broken stem that is inevitable on such a wind-prone plant.

Glad Tidings

This free-flowering floribunda produces masses of semi-double, high-centered flowers on a compact and bushy plant. The color is deep crimson, and with the dark, glossy green foliage behind can be a touch somber in poor light. Another drawback is its vulnerability to blackspot. It has plenty of impact, however, and the large number of high quality blooms will ensure that it continues to be widely planted. Bushy, compact growth makes it useful for many roles.

Size   Height: 2½ ft. Spread: 2 ft.
Flowering   Early to late summer
Uses   Beds, borders, hedge, exhibition
Scent   Some scent

Glad Tidings

Hannah Gordon

Hannah Gordon

This is one of those floribundas that you could mistake for a hybrid tea rose if you looked at just an individual bloom, although of course there are whole clusters of them. The white petals are delicately shaded cherry-pink at the edge, and the foliage is a glossy, deep bronze-green. A lovely rose for shape and coloring, and one with good disease resistance, but perhaps best appreciated at close viewing rather than as an eye-catching display across the garden.

Size   Height: 2½ ft. Spread: 2 ft.
Flowering   Early to late summer
Uses   Beds
Scent   Some scent

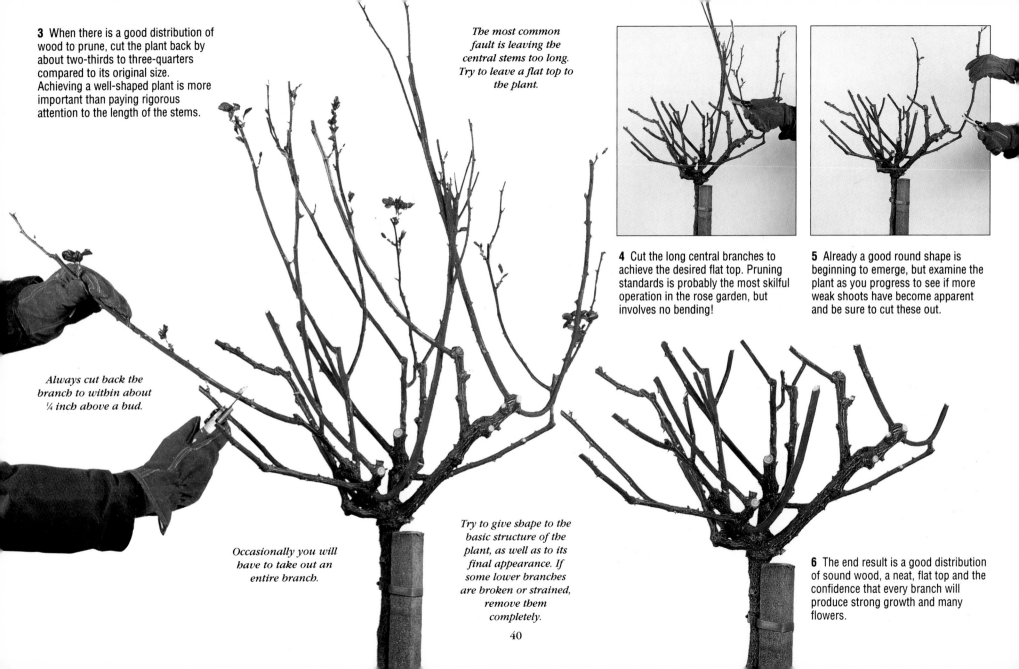

3 When there is a good distribution of wood to prune, cut the plant back by about two-thirds to three-quarters compared to its original size. Achieving a well-shaped plant is more important than paying rigorous attention to the length of the stems.

The most common fault is leaving the central stems too long. Try to leave a flat top to the plant.

4 Cut the long central branches to achieve the desired flat top. Pruning standards is probably the most skilful operation in the rose garden, but involves no bending!

5 Already a good round shape is beginning to emerge, but examine the plant as you progress to see if more weak shoots have become apparent and be sure to cut these out.

Always cut back the branch to within about ¼ inch above a bud.

Occasionally you will have to take out an entire branch.

Try to give shape to the basic structure of the plant, as well as to its final appearance. If some lower branches are broken or strained, remove them completely.

6 The end result is a good distribution of sound wood, a neat, flat top and the confidence that every branch will produce strong growth and many flowers.

40

Eye Paint

This is a real stunner, the sort of plant you will cross a garden to admire. "Eye Paint" is eye-catching, and produces flowers in such abundance that it can look more like a shrub rose than a floribunda. The whole plant is often a mound of brilliant blooms. The single flowers are scarlet with a white eye and golden stamens, and what they lack in size they make up for in numbers. Bear in mind its vigor: it grows tall and may be best in a shrub or mixed border, or as a hedge.

Size	Height: 4 ft. Spread: 3 ft.
Flowering	Early to late summer
Uses	Beds, borders, hedge
Scent	No fragrance

Eye Paint

Fragrant Delight

Fragrant Delight

This distinctive and outstanding rose has hybrid-tea-shaped blooms. Because these are so well shaped and occur in rather small clusters, it has been known for growers to list it as a hybrid tea. The color is difficult to describe, but light orange-salmon is close. As its name implies, fragrance is also a feature. The young leaves are a bronzy-green but mature to mid green and remain very shiny. This is one of the most popular floribundas, and is unlikely to disappoint.

Size	Height: 3-4 ft. Spread: 2 ft.
Flowering	Early to late summer
Uses	Beds, hedge, exhibition
Scent	Exceptional fragrance

Pruning A Patio Rose

Despite its relatively small size, the patio rose will require pruning in much the same way as its larger cousin, the bush rose. Many varieties rapidly accumulate twiggy wood which can be an impediment to healthy and productive growth. Because the buds are so small, it is difficult to prune to an eye, so reduce the plants by about two-thirds to three-quarters and concentrate on cleaning up the plant. Patio roses amply repay a little extra attention at pruning time in early spring. As most of them are grown in the confines of a pot or in a small area of soil, refurbishing them will encourage a significant improvement in the results the following summer. As long as the plant is growing in the correct type of container, it may not be necessary to use a larger one when repotting. Repot the rose by knocking the plant out of its container and carefully checking the drainage. Remove about 2 inches of soil at the base of the pot and place it with a standard potting soil from a garden shop. Then replace the plant and add a further 3 inches of the new compost at the top. If the rose is growing in a restricted border, remove the top 3 inches of soil and replace this with a good quality soil. Complete your spring program by giving the plants a good quality rose fertilizer. They need feeding like any other garden roses.

1 Check the pot for frost damage and scrub it clean if necessary. Repot the rose before pruning it. Start by removing any broken branches.

2 Patio roses may sustain quite a few broken branches. Once these have been eliminated, start to remove the twiggy growth and any dead material from the middle of the plant.

This wood can sometimes be used for cuttings in early spring.

For best results, trim the plant by about one-third in fall to reduce the risk of wind damage.

Do not be afraid to cut off any growth that the plant has made during the winter. It has probably been damaged by frost.

Make sure there is sufficient room in the pot to take water.

Plants grow well in earthenware pots. Roots stay cooler and are less likely to dry out.

Drummer Boy

This dwarf or patio rose is in a class of its own, difficult to beat for masses of unfading, brilliant crimson blooms. The color has a depth and brilliance that makes this a real eye-catcher. The growth habit of the bush is good, too, with a rounded shape and flowers on short branches that cover the plant from just above the ground upwards. The foliage matches the flowers: bright, shining and healthy, and, as you would expect, disease-resistant, too.

Size	Height: 1½-2 ft.
	Spread: 1½ ft.
Flowering	Early to late summer
Uses	Beds, patios, tubs, low hedge
Scent	Some scent

Drummer Boy

English Miss

English Miss

This pretty variety with camellia-like flowers, which are light rose pink but shade to white, will appeal to anyone seeking a delicate-looking rose that nevertheless has vitality and robustness . . . and a good fragrance for a floribunda. The large sprays, on a much-branching plant, contain many blooms, making this a good bedding rose. The foliage is a distinctive purplish-green verging to dark green. This is an interesting variety with a unique appeal.

Size	Height: 2½ ft. Spread: 2 ft.
Flowering	Early to late summer
Uses	Beds
Scent	Strong fragrance

Pruning a miniature rose

Most miniature roses are grown from cuttings, which means that they grow on their own roots and must be cut back quite severely each spring. The prunings can be used to make new plants. Pruning a miniature rose may seem an irksome task, but the results of cleaning up and cutting back quite hard are well worthwhile. Miniature roses also benefit from annual repotting.

3 Remove the last of the long growths, as shown here. Check that you have not missed any dead wood.

4 A perfectly repotted and well-pruned patio rose. A little bonemeal added to the top compost when repotting gives the rose a good start.

Below:
"Regensberg", a perfect small bush 12-18 inches tall, is an attractive patio rose that responds to the correct pruning.

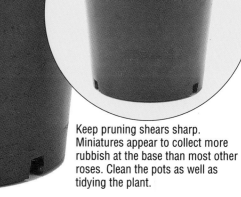

Keep pruning shears sharp. Miniatures appear to collect more rubbish at the base than most other roses. Clean the pots as well as tidying the plant.

Buck's Fizz

The color of this rose – a soft, clear orange – stands out from the dark green, glossy foliage, and the flowers look bright even when viewed across the garden. The buds have an attractive hybrid tea shape, adding to their beauty. Grow "Buck's Fizz" in beds where you want bright flowers on a medium to tall bush with an upright habit. Young leaves are reddish, and the foliage has the bonus of good disease resistance.

Size	Height: 3 ft. Spread: 2 ft.
Flowering	Early to late summer
Uses	Beds
Scent	Reasonably fragrant

Buck's Fizz

Conservation

Conservation

This award-winning floribunda is one of those dwarf plants sometimes described as patio roses. It is small enough to be grown in a patio bed or even in a pot. The fresh, coral pink color is shown off well by the backing of abundant glossy foliage, and there are plenty of flowers despite its small size. When the flowers open fully, the contrasting stamens are revealed to add another dimension to the display. A cheerful rose to add to your collection.

Size	Height: 1½ ft. Spread: 1 ft.
Flowering	Early to late summer
Uses	Beds, pots
Scent	Some fragrance

Rescuing A Neglected Plant

On average, you can expect to enjoy a well-tended garden rose for about 15 years, although this may be reduced to three or four years if a plant has been physically damaged, subjected to persistent disease or underfed. Some of these problems can be prevented and even remedied, given a program of good garden maintenance. Neglected plants normally fade away because they are supporting too much dead wood and have not been properly fed. Spring is the best time for dealing with old plants. However, it is often easier to identify a plant carrying a lot of dead wood during the early months of fall.

4 The shoots at the base of the plant may have grown late in the season and were not sufficiently mature to withstand a hard winter. Examine the center of the stem, or pith, which should be a bright white. If it is brown, it means the stem is frosted and should be cut down hard.

1 This is a typically tired plant, but it will soon respond to the correct pruning and care. Although pruning shears are being used here, do not attempt to cut out tough, dead wood with your best pruners. A saw is a safer and more effective tool for this sort of task.

2 Removing one or two old stumps can make a dramatic difference to the appearance of a neglected rose and makes the remaining fabric of the plant much easier to handle.

After removing a few old shoots, a neglected rose plant will revive rapidly.

This excess of twiggy wood may be the result of greedy cutting for flowers.

3 Some shoots only become evident after old stumps are eliminated. They are easily removed, but leave a clean cut that will not harbor disease.

5 Although much reduced, the fabric of the tree is still intact and with proper care will rapidly produce new growth as the season proceeds.

Bright Smile

As you might imagine from a name like this, it's a cheery, bright yellow rose with semi-double flowers, which do not fade. Its growth and height are very even so try it where you want a low-growing, cheerful rose, perhaps by the edge of a patio. You could even use it for a low internal hedge. It is little affected by weather and is very disease resistant, so you should have plenty of bloom and little trouble. A really good rose that has won awards in many countries.

Size	Height: 2 ft. Spread: 1½ ft.
Flowering	Early to late summer
Uses	Beds, front of borders, patios, low hedge
Scent	Some scent

Ard's Beauty

Ard's Beauty

The medium-sized, canary yellow flowers are pleasantly scented and carried in quite dense clusters on strong and bushy plants – useful qualities if you want a bedding rose. The leaves also show good disease resistance, which will cut down on the need to spray. The variety is not very widely grown so you may have to shop around for it, but the good fragrance and healthy growth make it worth including on your list.

Size	Height: 2½ ft. Spread: 2 ft.
Flowering	Early to late summer
Uses	Beds
Scent	Strong fragrance

Bright Smile

Seasonal Maintenance

1 Sometimes the stock on which the bush has been budded produces suckers. They are easy to recognize as they grow from below the ground and have a "wild" rose appearance.

2 If at all possible, try to remove the sucker by gently easing the ground and pulling the offending stem back to the main root system, where a good tug should solve the problem.

Although the rose is a very tolerant and adaptable plant, it will certainly respond to regular attention during the growing season, particularly feeding. If well-rotted farmyard manure is available, apply it as a heavy mulch in late winter or early spring. Immediately after pruning, apply a basic rose fertilizer according to the manufacturer's instruction, followed by a second application immediately after the first flush of flower. Never apply a rose food after midsummer. You can control weeds with a rose bed weedkiller or by lightly hoeing the ground. Never dig the soil in an established rose bed as this will damage and loosen the roots. If suckers appear from the wild rootstock, try to pull them out rather than cutting them off. Apart from feeding, the best thing you can do for your plants is to deadhead them. Removing the old flowering heads not only prevents the development of hips, but also encourages the continuity of flower and a stronger second flush. There are many sprays on the market to control pests and diseases but, fortunately, modern roses are quite resistant to these afflictions. If you do buy a spray, follow the instructions on the container closely and wash all the spray equipment thoroughly after use. As the season progresses, climbers and ramblers will produce new growth. Make sure that you tie these growths in securely to avoid exposing the plant to wind damage. When the first frosts arrive, cut your rose bushes down by one-third to reduce rocking during the winter.

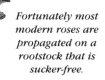

Fortunately most modern roses are propagated on a rootstock that is sucker-free.

This is the complete sucker shown being pulled out of the ground in the photographs.

3 Traditionally, gardeners assumed that all growths with seven leaves were suckers from briar rootstocks. This can be misleading, since many modern varieties have seven leaflets.

Many climbers and ramblers produce fresh young canes while flowering. Secure this growth loosely with soft string to avoid damage in summer storms. Bear in mind that this is a temporary measure and you should remove the ties in fall when you prune the plant and rearrange the structure.

Anne Harkness

This charming floribunda produces its spectacular sprays of pretty, semi-double, apricot-colored flowers on long stems – a useful attribute if you want it for a cut flower. It also has the significant bonus of flowering well late in the season – it is often at its peak in late summer, just when many other varieties are beginning to take a rest. It is a tall variety, so prune it fairly hard each year to prevent it becoming top-heavy.

Size	Height: 3-4 ft.
	Spread: 2 ft.
Flowering	Mid to late summer
Uses	Beds, borders, cutting, hedge
Scent	Some scent

Anne Harkness

Anna Livia

Anna Livia

A very appealing variety that you will probably want to grow for its bright color. The nicely formed and fragrant flowers are borne in handsome trusses, backed by semi-glossy foliage. The name, in case you are wondering, was James Joyce's name for the river Liffey in Ireland, but the color and fragrance are decidedly better in the rose! Although not strongly fragrant it has a pleasant scent. The plants are bushy and free-flowering.

Size	Height: 2½ ft. Spread: 2 ft.
Flowering	Early to late summer
Uses	Beds
Scent	Reasonably fragrant

1 All rose plants will benefit from a boost of fertilizer. Be sure to apply it before midsummer and take care not to let any fall on the base of the plant, as this could cause scorching.

2 Remember that hoeing the soil lightly not only removes weeds, but also improves the soil condition and helps to retain moisture. This is sometimes called a dust mulch.

If time is short, simply snap off the head. Developing hips discourage new growth

3 You can also suppress weeds and retain moisture by using a mulch of peat or peat substitute, such as pulverized bark. Apply when the soil is damp. There is little food in mulches.

4 When spraying, make sure that your applicator can reach under the foliage. This is as important as covering the top surface. Always follow the manufacturer's instructions.

5 Cut off the old rose head together with four leaves. Do not worry if this means removing buds, as these first few will only produce poor-quality bloom.

Amber Queen

The name says it all: beautifully formed amber-yellow flowers, highlighted against dark bronze foliage. While not the queen of all floribundas, it is one of the best in this color range. The short to medium height and bushy growth make this a fine bedding variety. It has good disease resistance, and the bonus of fragrance. This rose has won lots of awards in many countries, so you can be assured that it will put in a good performance.

Size	Height: 1½-2 ft.
	Spread: 2 ft.
Flowering	Early to late summer
Uses	Beds, exhibition
Scent	Reasonably fragrant

Amber Queen

Anisley Dickson

Anisley Dickson

The fact that this variety is named after a famous rose-breeder's wife is a good recommendation! The salmon-pink flowers have nicely shaped pointed blooms on well-spaced trusses, set off by dense, mid-green foliage. It is a very free-flowering variety that makes a nice cut flower as well as an attractive garden display. It tends to grow fairly tall, however, so this is not an ideal floribunda for a small garden unless you try it as a hedge.

Size	Height: 3 ft. Spread: 2 ft.
Flowering	Early to late summer
Uses	Beds, cutting, hedge
Scent	Some scent

Propagating Roses

Floribundas

Floribundas

Propagating Roses by Budding

Most modern roses are produced by budding or grafting the desired variety onto a vigorous rootstock, such as a wild briar or closely related species. This budding technique is carried out on millions of rose plants every year in nurseries. With care, there is no reason why you cannot achieve success with budding your own roses. You can obtain a briar from your local nursery and plant it during the spring. In midsummer, the briar should be big enough to take a bud. By the following spring, the new bud will sprout and produce a young branch 6-9 inches long by the middle of spring. If there are no late frosts, the branch will develop rapidly and the budded stock will form a rose bush in full flower by midsummer.

Cut the leaves back hard, leaving a short leaf stock which protects the bud inside.

1 Take good-quality budding wood from a stem that has recently flowered. Remove the flowering head together with the first three leaves.

2 Trim the leaves from the stem straight away; delay might cause the stems to shrivel. The bark must be firm and the sap should still be active.

Be sure to collect sticks of buds from healthy plants with no signs of disease or blemishes.

3 If not required immediately, store this stick of buds in a cool, moist atmosphere. Remove the thorns just before budding starts.

4 Cut a sliver of bark with a very sharp budding knife. The sliver should carry the bud, the leaf stock and as little wood as possible.

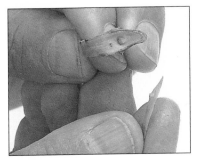

5 Reverse the sliver of bark and remove any wood that remains. It should come away easily. If not, it may be too dry and the bud will not "take".

6 Trim the base of the bark carrying the bud so that it looks neat and clean, and will slide snugly into the cut in the stock. This requires practice.

Stacey Sue

Try "Stacey Sue" if you want a pretty miniature with pink flowers and plenty of eye appeal. This is one of the prettiest miniatures, with rosette-type, soft pearl-pink flowers shading to a deeper color in the center. The tiny buds and flowers maintain the petite proportions so important in a miniature rose. It makes a neat plant and often grows to no more than about 12 inches tall. This excellent rose is good enough for showing.

Size	Height: 18 in. Spread: 12 in.
Flowering	Early to late summer
Uses	Patio beds and pots, exhibition
Scent	Some scent

Stacey Sue

Sweet Magic

Sweet Magic

This award winning rose is a super color. The medium-sized, semi-double flowers are exquisitely formed and a cheery, glowing orange with golden tints. Many of the miniatures lack a good scent, but this is delightfully fragrant. The plants are bushy with plenty of mid green, glossy foliage, and look like a scaled-down pretty floribunda. Being quite tall, however, it is one of those borderline miniatures described by some growers as a patio rose, by others as a miniature.

Size	Height: 18 in. Spread: 12 in.
Flowering	Early to late summer
Uses	Patio beds and borders
Scent	Strong fragrance

35

Preparing the rootstock

Remove some soil to reveal the main stem of the stock, or collar, and clean away any extraneous dirt. Make a T-shaped cut and gently prise the bark open to reveal the paler, sappy part inside. Do not cut too close to the top of the briar.

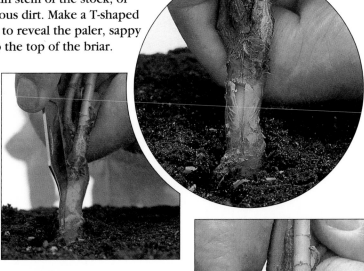

The leaf stock is not an essential part of the operation, but it does protect the bud and makes it easier to handle.

This big, fat bud has the potential to produce a first-class plant. If it appears black, discard it and start again.

7 A perfectly prepared bud implant ready for immediate insertion into the rootstock. The key to success is to work carefully but quickly.

8 Slide the prepared piece of bark carrying the bud into the cut made in the rootstock so that the implant fits neatly and the bud is uppermost.

9 You will need a length of pliable raffia about 15 inches long to hold the bud in place. Working from the bottom upwards, carefully tie the bud to the rootstock.

10 Wind the raffia around the budded stock until it covers the cut, with the bud exposed. Tie off. Keep the area as clean as possible.

Red Ace

Red Ace

An outstanding variety, with flowers good enough for exhibition. And although it may be listed as growing to 18 inches, it is often much more compact and frequently makes a plant no more than 12 inches tall. The dark, velvety-red flowers are medium-sized but perfectly formed. The growth is upright but compact and it makes a neat plant with mid green foliage. The proportions are pleasing, looking like a scaled-down, full-sized rose.

Size	Height: 18 in. Spread: 12 in.
Flowering	Early to late summer
Uses	Patio beds and pots, exhibition
Scent	No scent

Red Sunblaze

An excellent variety for the patio or perhaps a raised bed, "Red Sunblaze" has all the merits of "Orange Sunblaze". Like that variety it is a strong, healthy-looking large miniature with relatively big flowers that are bold and eye-catching. The color is a much darker and more intense red than "Orange Sunblaze", but the plant never looks drab. The light green, glossy foliage makes a good backdrop against which to see the flowers.

Size	Height: 18 in.
	Spread: 12 in.
Flowering	Early to late summer
Uses	Patio beds and pots
Scent	No scent

Red Sunblaze

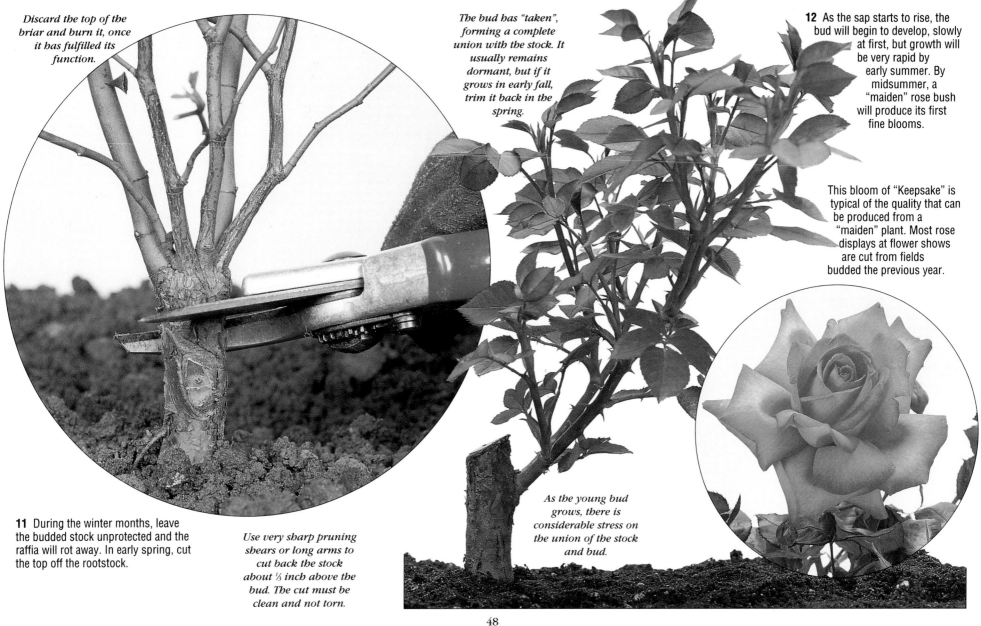

Discard the top of the briar and burn it, once it has fulfilled its function.

The bud has "taken", forming a complete union with the stock. It usually remains dormant, but if it grows in early fall, trim it back in the spring.

12 As the sap starts to rise, the bud will begin to develop, slowly at first, but growth will be very rapid by early summer. By midsummer, a "maiden" rose bush will produce its first fine blooms.

This bloom of "Keepsake" is typical of the quality that can be produced from a "maiden" plant. Most rose displays at flower shows are cut from fields budded the previous year.

As the young bud grows, there is considerable stress on the union of the stock and bud.

11 During the winter months, leave the budded stock unprotected and the raffia will rot away. In early spring, cut the top off the rootstock.

Use very sharp pruning shears or long arms to cut back the stock about ⅓ inch above the bud. The cut must be clean and not torn.

48

Orange Sunblaze

This was originally simply called "Sunblaze", but became "Orange Sunblaze" as there is now a whole range of colors in the series. This one is particularly bright and vivid, with double flowers in dazzling orange-scarlet. The blooms are long-lasting and quite large for a miniature, with the plants flowering freely over a long period. The plants have only average disease resistance, but are usually healthy and bushy. The foliage is light green and glossy.

Size	Height: 20 in. Spread: 12 in.
Flowering	Early to late summer
Uses	Patio beds and pots
Scent	Some scent

Orange Sunblaze

Peek A Boo

Peek A Boo

Try this one if you want a well-tried variety that keeps on performing well. The flower sprays are particularly graceful and pretty, the color varying between apricot and pink. With feeding and deadheading it will continue to flower throughout the summer. It makes a bushy plant, and is one of the best of its size. Under some conditions the plants do not exceed about 15 inches, but can grow taller. Some nurseries describe it as a miniature, others as a patio rose.

Size	Height: 18 in. Spread: 12 in.
Flowering	Early to late summer
Uses	Miniature gardens, patio beds and pots, rock garden
Scent	Reasonably fragrant

33

Propagating Roses by Taking Cuttings

This is the simplest way to take cuttings, but it does pose a few problems. Although roses can be grown from cuttings, the end results are not always successful because the modern rose has lost the ability to produce a satisfactory root system of its own. Recent research, however, has shown that this trend can be reversed and it seems that the newest roses, particularly ground cover varieties, will grow well from cuttings. Most species (wild) roses, old garden roses, many old ramblers and most miniature varieties will also prosper, but do not expect good results from modern hybrid teas and floribundas.

Prepare a piece of stem about 9 inches long with the lower cut trimmed just below a bud.

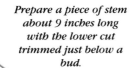

1 Old ramblers are easy to grow from cuttings. Take a stem that has recently flowered, usually just after midsummer, and remove the old head.

2 Trim all but two of the remaining leaves, slightly gouging out the buds to encourage roots to grow. Use a sharp knife. Collect propagating material from healthy stock.

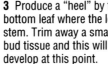

3 Produce a "heel" by trimming the bottom leaf where the leaf joins the stem. Trim away a small amount of bud tissue and this will cause roots to develop at this point.

4 You can dip the finished cutting in a solution to encourage root growth, but this is not essential. Whether you use rooting powder or liquid, read all the instructions carefully. Never allow the cutting to dry out.

5 Prepare a trench and add some sharp sand to the bottom. Place the cuttings in the trench so that each has about 1 inch of stem with two leaves above ground level.

6 The most common cause of failure with rose cuttings is dehydration, which happens if too much of the cutting protrudes above the soil. Providing the cuttings with semi-shade for the first few months also helps to avoid this problem.

Cinderella

Another tried and tested variety to consider if you want a miniature that does not grow tall – often it does not exceed 9 inches. The low and compact plant is well covered with abundant foliage and delicate-looking blooms. The tiny flowers are white flushed pink, and the fairly full petals give it the look of a scaled-down hybrid tea. It does well in a partially shaded position. It is worth shopping around to find this pretty rose.

Size	Height: 12 in. Spread: 9 in.
Flowering	Early to late summer
Uses	Miniature gardens, patio beds and pots, windowboxes
Scent	Some scent

Cinderella

Lavender Lace

Lavender Lace

This excellent variety is popular in the United States, with a lavender-pink color not often found in miniatures. The flowers are also very full and well formed, and reasonably fragrant – a decided bonus among miniatures, most of which lack scent. The flowers are freely produced over a long period. Unfortunately the variety is prone to blackspot.

Size	Height: 9 in. Spread: 6 in.
Flowering	Early to late summer
Uses	Miniature gardens, patio beds and pots, windowboxes
Scent	Reasonably fragrant

Breeding A New Rose

Almost every modern rose is the product of hybridization – the cross-fertilization of one rose with another. Growing the parent plants in a greenhouse, although not necessarily with heat, is best, as the summer season is not long enough to ripen the hips outdoors after fertilization. As they will be under glass for about 10 months, choose containers with about 5 gallons capacity. Select the parent plants and pot them on in early fall. A well-established two- or three-year-old potted plant will give a greater number of the necessary flowers and hips. Bring them into the greenhouse in midwinter, keeping them well-watered but not overfed. Even without heat they will flower in late spring. Hybridization can now begin and should be completed by early summer. After this, water sparingly and remove any extraneous growth. By late fall, the hips will be ripe and ready to harvest.

3 The most painstaking part of the operation is removing the stamens to create an all-female head. You must complete this before the pollen is ripe to prevent self-fertilization.

4 After removing the petals and stamens, wait for 24 hours. This allows time for the female stigmas to become receptive to fertilization.

You can tell when the stigma is receptive to fertilization because it appears sticky.

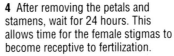

5 This is the delicate operation of cross-fertilization. Gently brush the pollen onto the ripe stigma. One application is more than enough.

1 Remove the petals cleanly by holding the calyx (the bottom part of the flower) with one hand and removing the petals with the other.

2 When you have removed the petals, you will be able to see the stamens. These are the male, pollen-bearing parts of the flower.

6 Once the operation is complete, allow the fertilized flower to develop in a dry atmosphere; it should ripen in about 4-5 months.

Baby Masquerade

If "Masquerade" the floribunda appeals to you, so will this scaled-down version, for it has the same magical coloring. The flowers can vary from yellow through pink to red, a multi-colored effect created because the individual blooms in a head change as they mature. And the more sunshine there is, the deeper the colors. This great favorite is very free-flowering, tough, and easy to grow. It is still a popular choice after more than 30 years.

Size	Height: 15 in. Spread: 8 in.
Flowering	Early to late summer
Uses	Patio beds and pots, windowboxes
Scent	Some scent

Baby Masquerade

Bush Baby

Bush Baby

For a real miniature to grow in a miniature garden, you need very compact varieties. "Bush Baby" is one of them, yet it's very hardy and healthy despite its diminutive size. The compact plants are also bushy and growth is so dense that you could use the variety to make a miniature hedge. The flowers are pale salmon pink, with a hint of yellow in the center. This is an outstanding variety among the smaller miniatures, with suprisingly bold flowers for its size.

Size	Height: 6 in. Spread: 4 in.
Flowering	Early to late summer
Uses	Miniature gardens, windowboxes
Scent	No scent

31

Breeding A New Rose by Raising Seed

Breeding a new rose is not complete until hips are harvested and the seed sown and successfully germinated into new plants. Remove the hips in late fall and store them in a cool, damp medium, such as damp peat or vermiculite for about three months. This enforced dormancy is necessary to induce the rose seeds to germinate. A short period of freezing also helps. In late winter extract the seeds from the hips and sow. Most seedlings produce flower by midsummer.

1 In order to raise healthy seedlings, use top-quality sterilized seed compost. Sow the seeds in pots or in a deep seed tray and firm the soil thoroughly.

Rose seed is not easy to germinate and you will need great patience. Protect the seeds from mice!

Always use clean seed trays and pots; good hygiene is essential.

2 Sow the seeds in an orderly way, leaving about 1 inch of space between them. Label them accurately so you can check the germination rate as the seedlings appear.

The lovely "Sheila's Perfume" was bred by an amateur hybridist.

3 Cover the seedlings with a layer of coarse sand about ½-inch thick. Rose seed takes a long time to germinate and this surface discourages the development of lichen.

A seed tray with ample drainage is essential. The greater the depth of soil, the better the quality of the seedlings produced.

4 Germination can be erratic. Seedlings of this size will take 6-8 weeks to grow and will produce flower after a further 3 weeks.

51

Angela Rippon

One of the best of the smaller miniatures. Often it grows to a height of only 12 inches, and looks like a charming, scaled-down version of a normal rose, with nicely shaped blooms like a hybrid tea rose, in a clear coral pink. The prettily shaped flowers have plenty of petals, and by miniature standards have a particularly good shape. Repeat flowering is also good, and because the plants are bushy and leafy they do not look too gaunt during spells without flowers.

Size Height: 15 in. Spread: 8 in.
Flowering Early to late summer
Uses Patio beds and pots, windowboxes, exhibition
Scent Some scent

Anna Ford

Anna Ford

The cheery, bright red "Anna Ford" has collected many awards as a patio rose. It is one of those plants on the borderline between being a miniature and a patio rose, and you may find it listed in catalogs under either heading, depending on the grower. Established plants have masses of flowers. And because the blooms last well when cut, this is one miniature with flowers large enough to make a useful contribution as a cut flower.

Size Height: 18 in. Spread: 12 in.
Flowering Early to late summer
Uses Patio beds and pots, cutting, miniature hedge
Scent Some scent

Angela Rippon

Flower Arranging

Miniature Roses

Showing Roses

Showing the fruits of your success in the garden can be a source of great pride. When selecting show blooms, remember healthy foliage can contribute just as much to a successful exhibit. In order to enhance the size of a bloom, give your roses an extra application of a nitrogenous feed – dried blood is best – in late spring. Before cutting any blooms, fill a large container with water and a compound available from garden centers or florists that encourages the cut flowers to take up water. Try to cut hybrid tea roses showing seven or eight petals about two days before exhibiting them. Plunge them into the prepared water and stand them in semi-darkness. They will grow in size but not develop. When transporting roses to a show, pack them tightly with other blooms or wrap them rolled in newspaper; never use tissue paper as it sticks to the blooms. On arrival at the show, give the blooms some time to develop and warm up. Cold petals are brittle and easily bruised. Remember to label your blooms clearly, which is bound to impress the judges.

Most hybrid tea bush roses develop side shoots. Remove these to allow the center bloom to grow bigger. This is called disbudding.

If half-opened blooms need a little encouragement to open out, coax them with a soft brush or manipulate them gently with your fingers.

"Elina" ("Peaudouce") is almost unbeatable if grown to perfection.

"Loving Memory" is a classic show bloom with a perfectly formed, high center.

Center: "Just Joey" can produce huge blooms.

A clean example of the pale "Polar Star" always attracts the judges.

Cut "Peace" young for showing.

"Keepsake's" high-pointed center makes it ideal for showing.

"Ingrid Bergman", a prolific, dark red rose, needs careful disbudding.

A typical example of a class for seven specimen HT blooms. Arrange them with care to achieve a balance of color and height.

52

Yellow Pages

This is a rose to grow if you want a dependable and easy-to-grow yellow rose that will put on a respectable show even in a wet season. It is nearly always in flower for the whole summer. The shape and form of the flowers is often less than perfect, but that does not matter if you just want a bright display in a bed. It also cuts well and can be useful for arrangements indoors. There are better yellow hybrid teas, but it is worth a place, and has good disease resistance.

Size	Height: 2½ ft. Spread: 2 ft.
Flowering	Early to late summer
Uses	Beds
Scent	Some scent

Yellow Pages

Whisky Mac

Whisky Mac

Although over 25 years old, this elegant-looking rose is still popular – the sign of a quality rose. The flowers are only medium-sized, but well-shaped on long stems, borne freely on neat, compact plants. The color is golden amber with bronze shading, and the foliage is also an attractive bronze-green verging to dark green. Add really strong fragrance, and you have a rose of outstanding merit. This is a first-class rose for general garden display.

Size	Height: 2½ ft. Spread: 2 ft.
Flowering	Early to late summer
Uses	Beds
Scent	Exceptional fragrance

Preparing Roses

If possible, pick roses early in the day when it is cool or in the evening, as this is when the plant is transpiring least. A rose picked in the middle of a hot summer day will rapidly wilt. All cut flowers benefit from a conditioning period, which simply means standing them in cool water for several hours before using them in a display. Remove any vicious thorns from the stems.

A mixture of long-stemmed hybrid tea roses picked from the garden.

Splitting the stem may make arranging the roses in florist foam a little more difficult.

Another method of increasing the surface area is to crush the lower part of the stem with a hammer or mallet. Make sure you do this on a wooden board or other solid surface.

When all the stems have been cut and prepared, stand the roses in a deep container with a small amount of cool (but not icy) water and leave them to drink for several hours or overnight to prolong their life.

Use a hammer or other heavy object, such as a rolling pin, to crush the stems.

Rather than just slicing across the stem, cut at a sharp angle and cut a slit a little way up the stem to reveal a larger surface area to help the rose take in water.

Valencia

This has to be on your shopping list if you are looking for a very fragrant, dark, almost orange-yellow rose. The large flowers are sometimes described as apricot-bronze with golden shadings, but however you describe them there is nothing wishy-washy about the color or the plant. The flowers are carried on vigorous shoots that are well-clothed with bronze-green, young leaves that mature to dark green. Disease resistance is good.

Size	Height: 2½ ft. Spread: 2 ft.
Flowering	Early to late summer
Uses	Beds
Scent	Strong fragrance

Valencia

Wendy Cussons

Wendy Cussons

This variety was all the rage 30 years ago. It is still one of the best roses for bedding (though its cerise color can clash with other varieties!). It has all the hallmarks of a classic rose: large, well-shaped blooms, prolific flowering, and an outstanding damask-type fragrance. The bushy, branching growth always makes a bed look well-filled. The flowers stand up well to wet weather and the foliage shows resistance to mildew.

Size	Height: 2½ ft. Spread: 2 ft.
Flowering	Early to late summer
Uses	Beds
Scent	Strong fragrance

Preventing Wilting

Occasionally a bunch of roses will wilt dramatically. This can be caused by stems drying out and then being unable to take up water properly. Always keep the stems of unused roses under water, even while you are working and arranging them.

2 Roll the bunch of roses tightly in some stiff paper and secure the wrapping with a rubber band. This also protects the roses during handling.

1 Recut all the stems at an angle and stand them immediately in a small amount of boiling water for about 2 minutes.

3 Stand the flowers in their wrapping in a container of cool water for several hours or until the roses have revived and look fresh.

Troika

A tried and tested variety that flowers freely, this is one to consider if the color combination appeals: apricot-orange with outer petals that are a deeper shade that is almost red. The long, pointed buds have a bronze tint, but acquire pink shades as they open. A distinctive flower that is not let down by lack of scent. You will also find the plant healthy and vigorous, with good disease resistance. It has luxuriant, bright green foliage and a vigorous, upright growth habit.

Size	Height: 2½ ft. Spread: 2 ft.
Flowering	Early to late summer
Uses	Beds
Scent	Strong fragrance

Troika

Tynwald

Tynwald

Creamy-colored roses are sometimes more beautiful than pure whites, especially with hybrid teas, where you can appreciate the subtleties of an individual bloom rather than the massed effect usually created by floribundas. "Tynwald" has big, cream blooms that shade to ivory at the heart. They contrast well with the luxuriant dark green foliage, which seems to remain largely free of diseases. The scent is pleasant but not particularly strong.

Size	Height: 3 ft. Spread: 2 ft.
Flowering	Early to late summer
Uses	Beds
Scent	Reasonably fragrant

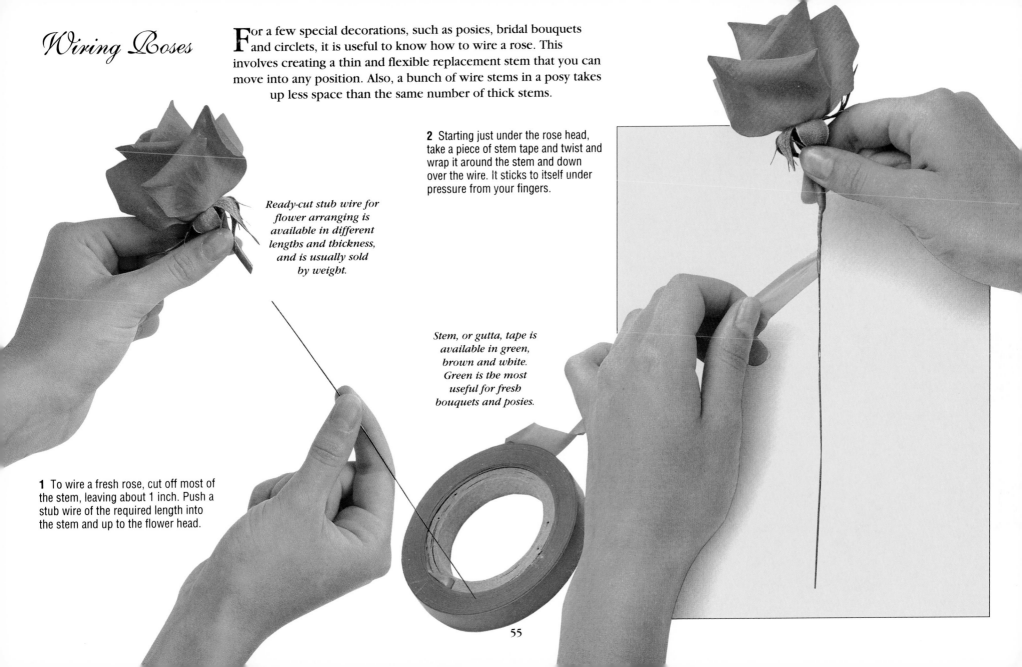

Wiring Roses

For a few special decorations, such as posies, bridal bouquets and circlets, it is useful to know how to wire a rose. This involves creating a thin and flexible replacement stem that you can move into any position. Also, a bunch of wire stems in a posy takes up less space than the same number of thick stems.

Ready-cut stub wire for flower arranging is available in different lengths and thickness, and is usually sold by weight.

2 Starting just under the rose head, take a piece of stem tape and twist and wrap it around the stem and down over the wire. It sticks to itself under pressure from your fingers.

Stem, or gutta, tape is available in green, brown and white. Green is the most useful for fresh bouquets and posies.

1 To wire a fresh rose, cut off most of the stem, leaving about 1 inch. Push a stub wire of the required length into the stem and up to the flower head.

Tranquillity

A beautiful rose to grow if the subtle combination of colors appeals. The flowers include shades of peach, apricot and cream, a fruity mixture matched by a pleasing perfume. The blooms are freely produced on strong stems, set off by dark green, glossy foliage. Try mixing it in a bed with deeper pinks and salmon-colored roses, and let the shades play against each other. The bushes are vigorous and trouble-free, with the bonus of good disease resistance.

Size	Height: 2½ ft. Spread: 2 ft.
Flowering	Early to late summer
Uses	Beds
Scent	Reasonably fragrant

Tranquillity

The Coxwain

The Coxwain

This is not a variety that you will find widely planted, but if the very attractive color appeals to you it is worth searching out because the scent is also good. The color is best described as a blend of creamy peach and orange-pink. The plant has a bushy growth habit that makes it useful for bedding. Its ancestry includes such famous roses as "Super Star" and "Silver Jubilee", and this shows in the quality of bloom coupled with a good scent.

Size	Height: 2½ ft. Spread: 2 ft.
Flowering	Early to late summer
Uses	Beds
Scent	Strong fragrance

Home-dried Roses

Drying roses at home is simple, and made even simpler if you have a constant source of warmth over which you can hang the drying flowers. A solid fuel cooker or kitchen range is ideal, but a boiler, airing rack or even a greenhouse will do. The aim is to dry the flowers quickly to preserve their color. They shrink quite a lot, but also open out a little after they have been hanging up. Either hang up roses complete with stems (as shown here) or cut fresh rose heads, leaving a small piece of stem, and attach a wire to them (see page 55). Hang them above the heat source, either singly or in a bunch. The wire will rust and bed tightly into the rose. As soon as the roses are thoroughly dried, remove them and store in a dark, dry place.

A fine bunch of fresh roses hanging up to dry.

The same roses, ready to use in an arrangement after drying.

These roses have been left to dry on their own stems.

Fairly full hybrid tea, floribunda or old-fashioned roses are the best for drying.

Scarlet-red and yellow roses are two of the best colors for drying.

56

Super Star

When it was launched over 30 years ago, this really was a superstar among roses. Nowadays, however, it has been overshadowed by newer varieties. If you like to follow stars of the past, however, then it certainly won't disappoint you. The neat, light vermilion flowers are more fragrant than many varieties that have followed it, with a distinct fruity aroma, and it remains a popular rose. A strong, healthy grower, it is an undemanding variety to grow.

Size Height: 4 ft. Spread: 2 ft.
Flowering Early to late summer
Uses Beds
Scent Strong fragrance

Super Star

Tequila Sunrise

Tequila Sunrise

You can't ignore this rose: the coloring of its wide, round flowers has all the promise of a glorious sunrise. The petals are deep gold at the base but heavily edged with vivid scarlet, giving the fully open bloom the impression of a red rose with a golden center. The glossy, mid-green leaves and sturdy growth habit combine to make this an impressive variety. Good disease resistance is another plus point. Pity it does not have a stronger scent.

Size Height: 2½ ft. Spread: 2 ft.
Flowering Early to late summer
Uses Beds
Scent Reasonably fragrant

A Selection of Roses for Arranging

The range and choice of garden roses is vast and bewildering, but this selection features some examples from many of the rose families which are suitable for arranging and display.

1 Hybrid tea "Ingrid Bergman".
2 Hybrid tea bush rose "Troika".
3 Floribunda bush rose "Picasso".
4 *Rosa rugosa* "F. J. Grootendorst".
5 Hybrid tea bush rose "Polar Star".

6 *Rosa rugosa alba*.
7 Modern shrub rose "Graham Thomas".
8 Floribunda bush rose "Intrigue".
9 Ground cover rose "Nozomi".
10 Old garden rose *R. Alba* "Félicité Parmentier".
11 Old garden rose *R. centifolia muscosa* "White Bath".
12 Hybrid tea bush rose "Royal Highness".
13 Hybrid tea bush rose "Blessings".
14 Old garden rose *R. gallica* "Charles de Mills".
15 Old garden rose *R. centifolia* "Petite de Hollande".
16 Climbing rose "Gloire de Dijon".
17 Old garden rose *R. bourboniana* "Honorine de Brabant".
18 Hybrid tea bush rose "Grandpa Dickson".

19 Wild rose species *Rosa webbiana*.
20 Hybrid tea bush rose "Heart Throb" ("Paul Shirville").
21 Wild rose species *Rosa eglanteria* (Sweetbriar).
22 Hybrid tea bush rose "King's Ransom".
23 Floribunda bush rose "Chinatown".
24 Old garden rose hybrid perpetual "Souvenir de Dr Jamain".
25 Old garden rose *Rosa gallica* "Officinalis" (Apothecary's rose).
26 Hybrid tea bush rose "Fragrant Charm 84" ("Royal William").
27 Old garden rose *R. alba* "Königin von Dänemark" ("Queen of Denmark").
28 Rambler rose "Francis E. Lester".
29 Rambler rose "Seagull".
30 Miniature rose *R. rouletti*.
31 Floribunda bush rose "The Queen Elizabeth Rose".
32 Old garden rose *R. alba* "Celeste" ("Celestial").

Stella

Sunset Song

You will probably want to grow this variety because you like its interesting and beautiful coloring. The well formed flowers are an unusual, rich golden amber, though at times the color verges on bronze. The flowers are carried singly or in clusters on strong stems, and it makes an attractive cut flower. The growth is vigorous, but the plant usually remains in the medium height range so it is still suitable for rose beds in a small garden.

Size	Height: 2½ ft. Spread: 2 ft.
Flowering	Early to late summer
Uses	Beds, cutting
Scent	Some scent

Sunset Song

Stella

This old rose is not so widely grown nowadays, but it should not be forgotten, because is has superb coloring and flowers that resist rain well. The petals are creamy pink, edged carmine, creating a pretty shading effect as the bloom opens. The vigorous growth is rather upright and the flowers tend to be carried in clusters at the top of unbranched stems. It is prone to blackspot, which may account for its decline in popularity.

Size	Height: 3 ft. Spread: 2 ft.
Flowering	Early to late summer
Uses	Beds
Scent	Some scent

A Classic Porcelain Vase

The painted flowers on this porcelain vase provide the cue for what to put in it and the best colors to choose. Roses have been mixed with complementary garden flowers and foliage, and the effect of the whole arrangement is harmonious and pretty.

Recut flower stems, then split any woody ones and trim away lower foliage.

The roses are old-fashioned and modern types. The multi-petaled old roses have the right feel for this traditional look.

In this arrangement, keep the amount of foliage to a minimum to leave space for plenty of different flower varieties.

2 Arrange the tall stems first in a fan shape across the back of the vase to create an outline and add a trailing stem at one side.

Replace shorter-lived flowers as they fade to give the arrangement a longer life.

3 Continue filling in the display with shorter stems of phlox, alstroemeria and roses. Position them so that they are evenly spaced throughout and near to the front.

1 Tape a block of damp floral foam securely into the vase, leaving it proud of the rim. Add more water as a reservoir to sustain the flowers. Bunch the flowers to see how the colors work together.

4 Complete the arrangement with filler material, such as *Alchemilla mollis* and small-flowered, scented white "Seagull" roses. Let a few flowers curve naturally down to the table.

Simba

Bright yellow, perfectly shaped flowers give this rose the look of a classic. And the mid-green foliage on bushy plants makes a good backdrop against which to view the flowers. Strong stems, a bright color, attractive foliage and a long vase life, make this a good variety for cutting, as well as for garden display. It is only let down by its unremarkable fragrance, but for garden display massed in a bed its compact habit, bright color and quality flowers make this an ideal yellow.

Size	Height: 2½ ft. Spread: 2 ft.
Flowering	Early to late summer
Uses	Beds, cutting, exhibition
Scent	Reasonably fragrant

Simba

Solitaire

Solitaire

This is one to think about if you have space for a tall variety. Its well-formed, high-centered, exhibition-sized flowers are dark yellow edged pink – a distinctive and beautiful combination. This very healthy and robust variety has many merits, but unfortunately it tends to be too tall for bedding in a small garden. It is not a widely grown rose, perhaps because most people are looking for more compact varieties these days, but worth a place if you are looking for quality blooms.

Size	Height: 4 ft. Spread: 2½ ft.
Flowering	Early to late summer
Uses	Beds, borders, exhibition
Scent	Reasonably fragrant

Pink Roses in An Elegant Glass Vase

This curved glass vase makes any flower displayed in it look elegant. However, its narrow neck means that only a few stems can fit in it, so choose roses with large flower heads for maximum effect.

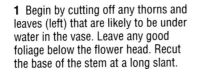

1 Begin by cutting off any thorns and leaves (left) that are likely to be under water in the vase. Leave any good foliage below the flower head. Recut the base of the stem at a long slant.

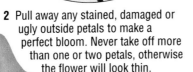

2 Pull away any stained, damaged or ugly outside petals to make a perfect bloom. Never take off more than one or two petals, otherwise the flower will look thin.

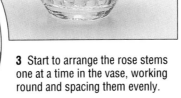

3 Start to arrange the rose stems one at a time in the vase, working round and spacing them evenly.

4 Add more blooms (right) to create a cluster of flower heads in a curving shape that reflects the curves of the base below. Loosen the heads so that they are not crushed and have a little air and space around them.

Make the arrangement an all-round one to be viewed from any angle.

If the stems are slightly short for the vase, fill the base with clear glass marbles.

Savoy Hotel

The big flowers match the grandeur of the name. The large, well-shaped blooms are pastel pink with deeper shades in the center of the flower. The foliage is also big and bold and the plants always look well-clothed, and a good shape as they tend to branch well from the base. If you want a hybrid tea with massive flowers, borne in profusion and also good for *en mass* viewing in a bed, this should be on your short-list. The plant shows good disease resistance.

Size	Height: 2½ ft. Spread: 2 ft.
Flowering	Early to late summer
Uses	Beds, exhibition
Scent	Reasonably fragrant

Savoy Hotel

Silver Jubilee

This is a well-established variety that has managed to remain popular though the years. This has more to do with its coloring than its nicely shaped blooms: a merging of apricot, pink and cream with subtle shading between. The variety has other qualities, such as strong vigor and healthy, very disease-resistant foliage. A good variety to choose if you want a rose that is dependable, strongly scented, and has a strong yet subtle coloring.

Silver Jubilee

Size	Height: 2½ ft. Spread: 2 ft.
Flowering	Early to late summer
Uses	Beds, exhibition
Scent	Strong fragrance

Roses, Carnations and Eucalyptus

The blue-green eucalyptus leaves make a perfect foil for the strong crimson-red spray carnations and long-stemmed roses. Use a simple, plain glass vase that will not detract attention from the flowers.

1 Trim off lower stems and leaves from each spray of eucalyptus and cut all stems to the same length. Begin to put them into the vase, working round in a circle.

2 With the eucalyptus in place, add carnations throughout the foliage, working evenly all over the arrangement. Use some shorter stems at the outer edges.

3 Finally add the roses, spacing them out equally throughout the arrangement between the carnations. Aim to create a smooth, continuous outline above the vase.

Saint Hugh's

It is worth searching out this fairly uncommon variety, for it has really attractive and well formed flowers in beautiful shades of creamy yellow, deepening to gold and with the outer petals sometimes tipped pink. Some gardeners do not like the pale colors, such as whites and creams, but this one has enough yellow to make it bold, and the shading adds interest. It is a bushy grower and makes a surprisingly bold bedding rose when the flowers are set off by good foliage.

Size	Height: 2½ ft. Spread: 2 ft.
Flowering	Early to late summer
Uses	Beds
Scent	Reasonably fragrant

Saint Hugh's

Sarah

Sarah

You may also find this rose sold as "Jardins de Bagatelle" (as its alternative name implies, the rose was raised by a French nursery). It deserves to be better known, both for garden decoration and as a cut flower. Like many roses, the blooms have a combination of colors that vary as they age and are difficult to describe. It is basically a cream-colored rose with light pink on the extreme edges of the petals, giving the bush a light and cheery appearance. The scent is good, too.

Size	Height: 3 ft. Spread: 2 ft.
Flowering	Early to late summer
Uses	Beds
Scent	Strong fragrance

Roses in a Jelly Mold

This informal arrangement uses scented roses and honeysuckle displayed in an old-fashioned jelly mold. Be open to new ideas when you come to select a vase, and look through your kitchen cupboards for unusual containers.

These are blooms from the delicately colored floribunda rose, "Café".

1 Push a block of foam into the container and mark where to cut it. Leave it slightly proud of the rim to allow more height for arranging.

2 Remove the foam and slice it cleanly through with a sharp kitchen knife. Then wet the foam and push it tightly back into the container.

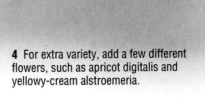

3 Begin to fill in the foam with stems of honeysuckle. Spread them all over the arrangement, spacing them out as evenly as possible.

4 For extra variety, add a few different flowers, such as apricot digitalis and yellowy-cream alstroemeria.

Royal William

This is not such a strong red as "Ingrid Bergman", and lacks the color intensity of that rose, but it has a stronger fragrance. It nevertheless has beautiful bright red blooms, freely produced on strong stems. It performs well in wet years as well as dry ones, and is the kind of reliable rose that should give many years of pleasure for the minimum of effort. The plentiful dark green foliage looks lush and gives the bushes an appearance of vigor and health.

Size	Height: 3 ft. Spread: 2 ft.
Flowering	Early to late summer
Uses	Beds
Scent	Strong fragrance

Left and above left: Royal William

Ruby Wedding

With a name like this, the variety is sure to be popular with anyone looking for a gift for that special occasion. The color matches the image of romance: rich, ruby red with a velvety look. The flowers are carried on stiff, upright stems, which make it a good rose for cutting. It looks good in traditional rose beds, but do not hesitate to try it in mixed borders – think about planting it in small groups for a splash of color.

Size	Height: 2½ ft. Spread: 2 ft.
Flowering	Early to late summer
Uses	Beds, borders, cutting
Scent	Some scent

Right and above right: Ruby Wedding

Felicia Roses in a Wire Basket

This simple arrangement of pale pink hybrid "Felicia" musk roses is very quick to make. The moss lining inside the basket disguises the foam. Either use suitable moss from the garden or buy it from a florist or garden center. Stand the finished arrangement on a mat to collect any drips of water.

1 Soak some sphagnum moss in water until it is completely wet and then squeeze it until it is just damp. Line the base and the sides of the basket.

2 Use a small cylinder of florist foam or cut a piece to fit snugly inside the basket. Make the foam wet and push it into place inside the moss lining.

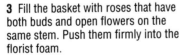

3 Fill the basket with roses that have both buds and open flowers on the same stem. Push them firmly into the florist foam.

4 Continue filling the basket until you have a full, rounded outline of roses. Regularly mist it with a fine spray to keep both the moss and roses fresh.

The subtle pale pink hybrid musk rose "Felicia" is generous with both blooms and scent.

Rosy Cheeks

The crimson and gold color combination makes this rose something special, with the large flowers creating a distinctive and pleasing color contrast. But the variety has many merits in addition to color: the large, perfectly-shaped flowers are freely produced, with prolific repeat flushes, and enhanced by a terrific scent. Combined with vigorous growth and good disease resistance, these are all the qualities associated with a first-rate bedding rose.

Size	Height: 2½ ft. Spread: 2 ft.
Flowering	Early to late summer
Uses	Beds
Scent	Exceptional fragrance

Rosy Cheeks

Royal Romance

Royal Romance

A delightful salmon-peach rose, and still one of the best varieties of this color. The large flowers are beautifully formed, though they tend to be a bit loose when open, and are borne in profusion over a long period. The compact plants remain neat and bushy, and the dark leaves, which have good disease resistance, almost always look lush and healthy. Although not widely grown, it is a pretty flower and makes a nice bedding rose.

Size	Height: 2½ ft. Spread: 2 ft.
Flowering	Early to late summer
Uses	Beds
Scent	Reasonably fragrant

"Albertine" Roses in a Basket

Every kind of basket, whether it is smooth and shiny or rough and twiggy, has an affinity with roses. The popular rambler "Albertine", with its lax stems and drooping pale pink heads, looks entirely at home in this small twig basket.

1 Plunge a block of floral foam under water and hold it there until it no longer bobs above the surface, or as specified by the manufacturer.

2 Make the basket waterproof by lining it with clear plastic or foil. Place the damp foam block in the center of the basket.

3 Working around methodically, arrange roses at the base of the basket, positioning them so their heads droop gently over the rim.

4 Fill the center of the basket, leaving the top of the handle clear. Aim for a natural, tumbling effect as shown above.

Red Devil

This variety will appeal to anyone who exhibits roses, but that does not diminish its usefulness as a decorative rose for beds and borders. The large, light red blooms of this bush are exceptionally shapely, with lots of petals. The shape is a classic hybrid tea form, and the variety is an excellent choice if you want to try your hand at exhibiting in the local show, even if you are a beginner. The plant shows good disease resistance, but the large flowers are easily damaged by rain.

Size	Height: 4 ft. Spread: 3 ft.
Flowering	Early to late summer
Uses	Beds, borders, exhibition
Scent	Reasonably fragrant

Red Devil

Rosemary Harkness

Rosemary Harkness

This is a good bedding rose that creates a subtle yet colorful display with flowers that harmonize and fuse shades of salmon, orange and yellow, though this depends on age. Its branching habit makes it useful for bedding, but it will also make an attractive low hedge. Its sweet fragrance has helped to make it a popular choice with gardeners looking for a good general garden display coupled with scent. Try cutting some blooms for the home.

Size	Height: 3 ft. Spread: 2 ft.
Flowering	Early to late summer
Uses	Beds, cutting, hedges
Scent	Strong fragrance

18

Mixed Roses in a Basket

Old-fashioned, scented roses with wonderful full-petaled heads in dense shades of raspberry, crimson and deep, glowing pinks are especially suitable for filling country-style baskets.

1 Aluminum foil is excellent for lining a deep basket as it is easier to mold up the sides than plastic. It will provide a durable and waterproof "container" within the basket. However, take care not to tear it as you put it in place.

The pale mauve rose is "Fantin-Latour", a beautiful, highly scented tall Centifolia rose.

2 Drop a block of damp florist foam into the basket. A piece this size will not need taping, but you may need to wedge in smaller pieces of foam to fill in any gaps.

3 Fill the basket with roses, starting at the front edge and working across methodically. The roses at the back should be slightly taller than those at the front of the display.

The light crimson R. gallica "Officinalis", also known as the Apothecary's rose, is the plain mutation of Rosa Mundi.

Try to mix lighter and darker shades of red and pink as much as possible for emphasis and contrast.

4 The finished basket looks best when viewed from the front, so display it at any height quite close to a wall or against a background feature. Stand it on a mat in case moisture leaks through, and top up the foam with a regular spray of water.

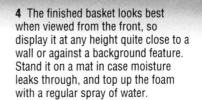

Princess Royal

This recently introduced variety has medium to large, high-centered flowers packed with petals on strong, bushy plants. The golden apricot flowers with a hint of bronze have the merit of good weather resistance, and there's the bonus of a mild but pleasing spicy fragrance. The mid-green foliage is semi-glossy, and like many of the best modern varieties, has good disease resistance. The color should combine well if interplanted with blues such as lavender or catmint.

Size	Height: 3 ft. Spread: 2 ft.
Flowering	Early to late summer
Uses	Beds
Scent	Reasonably fragrant

Princess Royal

Rebecca Claire

Rebecca Claire

This is one of those varieties that deserves to be better known and grown more often. It has won several awards, including one for scent, although not everyone agrees that this rose is particularly outstanding when it comes to scent. The coral pink blooms, with pretty veining on the outer petals, are very appealing and are undoubtedly the main reason for growing the variety. They are freely produced on bushy plants, making this a good bedding variety.

Size	Height: 3 ft. Spread: 2 ft.
Flowering	Early to late summer
Uses	Beds
Scent	Strong fragrance

Roses and Peonies

There is a point in early summer when the old-fashioned shrub roses are in full bloom alongside the extravagant flowers of herbaceous peonies. As both species are multi-petaled and are found in a similar range of colors, the two flowers look wonderful mixed together in relaxed arrangements. They also last the same length of time when cut.

1 Crumple a square of wire netting so that it fits inside the bowl. Tape it in place if you wish. Large-headed flowers with stems cut short are top-heavy and therefore need the support of wire in their container.

Use small-scale wire netting from a hardware store or buy special plastic-covered wire from a florist.

2 Cut each stem so that it is short enough to slot into the wire yet leaves the flower head sitting just above the rim.

Roses with a full cup shape and rich pink coloring, such as "Constance Spry", are ideal for this display.

4 When you have used up all the blooms and the display is finished, give the flowers a light misting of water to keep them fresh.

Use a peony such as a double pink "Sarah Bernhardt".

3 Begin by putting one flower at a time into the bowl, pushing the stem through the wire mesh. Work carefully round the bowl, keeping the blooms quite tight together. Mix the shades of pink and red throughout for maximum contrast.

5 The finished arrangement would look good below eye-level on a low table or as a dining table decoration.

Precious Platinum

This is a rose grown primarily for its bright crimson color. It lacks the traditional high-centered flowers of the classic hybrid teas, but they are borne prolifically in clusters and this gives them the sort of display associated with most floribunda roses. Vigorous, branching growth also helps to make this a good bedding rose. Once established it makes a good show from a distance. Although disease resistance is reasonably good, mildew can sometimes be a problem.

Size	Height: 2½ ft. Spread: 2 ft.
Flowering	Early to late summer
Uses	Beds
Scent	Some scent

Prima Ballerina

Precious Platinum

Prima Ballerina

The very fragrant flowers of this old variety are deep rose-pink. The large blooms, famed for their scent, show good weather resistance and are carried on strong stems. The glossy foliage shows some disease resistance, but you may find it prone to mildew. Although it makes a vigorous bush, with an upright growth habit, flowering can be patchy by late summer. There are more reliable modern varieties, but there is still a place for this old favorite.

Size	Height: 3 ft. Spread: 2 ft.
Flowering	Early to late summer
Uses	Beds, exhibition
Scent	Exceptional fragrance

A Jug of Climbing Roses

Choose rose stems overloaded with blooms and cram them haphazardly into a tall jug for a beautifully informal arrangement.

1 Cut the flowering stems off the very long trailing laterals of rambler roses, such as this "Seagull".

2 Snip off any faded flowers, the lower stems and foliage. Place the tallest stems in the jug first (left).

3 Fill in any gaps with the shorter stems, making sure a good all-round arrangement is achieved.

Polar Star

As the name implies, this is a white variety, but with a strong suggestion of cream. The blooms have a particularly good shape, with a high center and long, pointed buds. The variety is exceptionally free-flowering, and the dark green foliage makes a good backdrop against which to view the white blooms. The plants are vigorous, with tall, upright growth. Disease resistance is good, making this a white with few faults.

Size	Height: 4 ft. Spread: 2 ft.
Flowering	Early to late summer
Uses	Beds, exhibition
Scent	Reasonably fragrant

Polar Star

Pot o'Gold

Pot o' Gold

This is a good choice if you want a yellow hybrid tea variety with good fragrance for massed planting. It has perfectly shaped flowers, with high centers, borne singly and in trusses, which ensures a steady flow of blooms and plenty of color. The flowers are a golden yellow appropriate to the name. The compact growth and semi-glossy leaves, coupled with good disease resistance, make this a useful all-round bedding variety.

Size	Height: 2½ ft. Spread: 2 ft.
Flowering	Early to late summer
Uses	Beds
Scent	Strong fragrance

15

Old Roses in Blue and White China

The long, curving stems of many of the small-flowered species and hybrid climbing roses may not seem suitable for a vase, but make lovely, if short-lived displays in shallow bowls or similar containers.

1 Recut the stems at an angle (right) and cut off and clear away any of the lower foliage and thorns that will be below the water level in the container.

2 Choose compatible containers in a range of shapes and sizes. Divide the roses into different types and put each type in a separate container.

3 Place the second variety in a different container (left). Keep the roses with the longest stems for the tallest jug or vase.

4 Position the three arrangements with the tallest at the back. Leave enough space around them so that each is clear to see, but together they make a harmonious single group as shown below.

Use crumpled wire or florist foam if the roses are difficult to arrange in a bowl of this shape.

67

Piccadilly

If you like bi-colored roses, try "Piccadilly", and do not be put off by the fact that it was introduced over 30 years ago. It is an exciting confection of scarlet and gold with beautiful, high-pointed buds. It is seen at its best in cool weather: the reds and yellows tend to merge and have less punch in hot sunshine; a similar effect occurs as the flowers age. The coppery foliage is abundant and disease-resistant. Although it has dropped in popularity, it is still available.

Size	Height: 2½ ft. Spread: 2 ft.
Flowering	Early to late summer
Uses	Beds
Scent	Some scent

Piccadilly

Pink Favorite

Pink Favorite

Another rose that is not as widely grown as it deserves, but well worth including in the garden if you want a rose-pink variety for exhibition or simply as a bright bedding display. The high-centered flowers have bright pink petals, slightly darker on the outside than the inside. It is not very fragrant, but that drawback is offset by its excellent disease resistance. Mildew and blackspot are seldom a problem on this excellent variety.

Size	Height: 2½ ft. Spread: 2 ft.
Flowering	Early to late summer
Uses	Beds, exhibition
Scent	Some scent

Yellow Roses in A Pink Glazed Bowl

Traditionally, the classic rose bowl for displaying roses is round and quite shallow, with a gently curving outline. However, it is not easy to support roses with heavy heads in a bowl of this shape, so you may need to add crumpled chicken wire or plastic-coated netting. Mix in another type of flower or foliage to conceal the mesh. Here, acid green *Alchemilla mollis* complements rich yellow "Graham Thomas" roses.

1 Begin by cutting out a rough circle of small- to medium-sized wire netting with wire cutters. Make the circle slightly larger than the area of the top of the bowl.

3 Add sprays of *Alchemilla* to the bowl, covering the wire and creating a soft, curving outline. The *Alchemilla* can extend beyond the edge of the bowl to make a wide, low display.

The pink sponged glaze on the 1950s bowl is an effective foil to the green and yellow flowers.

2 Squeeze the wire a little so that it drops easily into the bowl and rests about halfway down. If it does not feel secure, attach it firmly to the inside of the bowl with florist's tape.

4 Space the roses evenly throughout the arrangement, in between the foliage. Leave the center stems a little longer than those around the lower edge. Give a fine mist of water.

5 This arrangement would look good as the centerpiece of a dining table or on a low table to be viewed from above.

"Graham Thomas" is a good choice of rose as a cut flower as it keeps it color well and has pretty cup-shaped blooms.

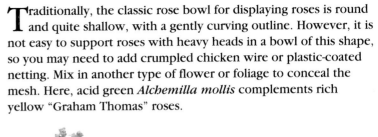

Peer Gynt

Despite being over 20 years old, "Peer Gynt" is still a cheery and worthwhile rose to have in the garden. At first sight it looks something like a loose "Peace" when fully open. The large, rounded flowers are yellow with the petals lightly shaded pink at the edges, more noticeable as they age in hot sun. If you like a traditional hybrid tea shape, you may find the flowers too open-cupped. The foliage is dark and growth strong and vigorous. Unfortunately it is prone to mildew.

Size	Height: 2½ ft. Spread: 2 ft.
Flowering	Early to late summer
Uses	Beds
Scent	Some scent

Peer Gynt

Peggy Netherthorpe

Peggy Netherthorpe

Although not widely available, "Peggy Netherthorpe" is a beautiful fuchsia pink rose with classic hybrid tea shape: large flowers with a high pointed center, on long, strong stems. This makes it an excellent exhibition variety. It makes an elegant cut flower too, useful in vases or arrangements, and it lasts well in water. It grows rather tall for a small garden and unfortunately lacks good disease resistance, being prone to mildew.

Size	Height: 3½ ft. Spread: 2 ft.
Flowering	Early to late summer
Uses	Beds, exhibition
Scent	Reasonably fragrant

13

Rose Table Decoration

Some people simply cannot bring themselves to cut a rose with a very short stem. However, once you have come to terms with the idea, you can begin to make all kinds of unexpected and unusual decorations and arrangements in a variety of containers.

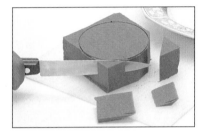

1 Cut a piece of foam to the right thickness for the dish then mark out a circle by pressing a round object into the foam. Cut out the foam to shape using a sharp kitchen knife.

2 Wet the foam as usual and push it onto a pin holder, as here, or use a special foam holder. An old-fashioned pin holder is good and heavy. A foam holder will need to be taped in place.

3 Position the damp foam in the center of the plate and cut all the flowers short, so that the stems are only about 2 inches long. Put the first rose in the center.

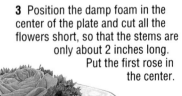

Arrange a ring of cornflowers right around the central rose, followed by a ring of scabious.

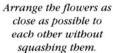

Arrange the flowers as close as possible to each other without squashing them.

4 Make a ring of flowers outside the cornflowers (above), pushing the stems into the foam to secure them. The delicate mauve of these blooms blends pleasingly with the bright blue of the cornflowers.

5 Finish with a final ring of roses, which simply sits inside the rim of the dish. Top up the dish with water for the roses and to keep the foam damp.

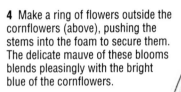

Peace

Any rose that is still as popular as this one after more than 45 years of competition from other excellent varieties must be something special. The flowers are big and beautiful; for sheer flower size difficult to beat. The coloring is attractive, too: creamy yellow petals with a ruffled edge, shading to light pink. The strong stems make it good for cutting, and the tall, wide bushes do not look amiss in a mixed border. Sadly it is let down by poor fragrance.

Size	Height: 4 ft. Spread: 3 ft.
Flowering	Early to late summer
Uses	Beds, borders, cutting, exhibition
Scent	Some scent

Peace

Peaudouce

Peaudouce

This is a rose of distinction, with its pale primrose-yellow flowers, changing to cream with age, and classic hybrid tea shape and proportions, with a high pointed center. Although it makes a fine bedding plant, the quality of the blooms puts it among the exhibition-quality varieties. The flowers tend to be borne singly on long stems, making it a good cut flower. The whole plant usually looks healthy and vigorous, and disease resistance is good.

Size	Height: 3 ft. Spread: 2 ft.
Flowering	Early to late summer
Uses	Beds, cutting, exhibition
Scent	Strong fragrance

Roses in Tea Cups

A very simple but effective way of using garden roses is to line up a row of three, four or five cups and saucers and use them as small vases to hold single blooms or little bunches of your favorite roses. The finished group can stand in a line along a shelf or windowsill or down the center of a table.

1 Choose an attractive group of cups and saucers and fill them with water. Select appropriate roses for each cup.

2 Make small arrangements in each cup, adding a few pieces of foliage to one or two if you wish. You can mix different varieties or keep to a single type.

3 Arrange the cups, balancing light and dark flowers along the line and mixing solid color cups with lighter, floral-sprigged ones.

Cut stems to the right length and remove any unwanted foliage.

Split the stems from the base to help the roses take up water.

Painted Moon

This is one of those modern hybrid tea roses that is almost as good as a floribunda for massed bedding. The rather flat but full-petaled flowers are primrose deeply flushed with scarlet and pink. Like most roses, the shades intensify and change as the blooms age. The growth is neat and compact, and the leaves have good disease resistance. This is the kind of hybrid tea to be enjoyed as individual blooms or massed for a colorful display in a bed.

Size	Height: 2½ ft. Spread: 2 ft.
Flowering	Early to late summer
Uses	Beds
Scent	Reasonably fragrant

Painted Moon

Painted Moon

Paul Shirville

Paul Shirville

This is a variety with the attributes of a first-rate hybrid tea: a good shape, interesting coloring, and a strong scent. The pink blooms incorporate shades of peach, creating a sort of salmony effect that is particularly appealing. The bushy and rather spreading growth, with plenty of disease-resistant foliage, makes it a good bedder. Try cutting some of the flowers to take indoors so that you can more easily appreciate its many virtues.

Size	Height: 2½ ft. Spread: 2½ ft.
Flowering	Early to late summer
Uses	Beds, cutting
Scent	Strong fragrance

Roses in Clear Glass

Sometimes you need to make a table decoration or arrangement for a room quickly and nothing could be faster to put together than this idea. It relies on sparkling clean and shiny glass, so the first thing to do is to spend a few minutes buffing the glass until it glitters. Pour the water in carefully in order not to splash the sides and create tide marks or spots on the glass.

1 Prepare each rose by cutting the stem away from the rose head at the point where the stem fattens out into the flower. A good solid rose such as "Graham Thomas" is best for this treatment.

"Graham Thomas" is one of the new breed of English roses, old-fashioned in style but repeat-flowering.

2 The water should be just deep enough to allow the flowers to float easily. Lay the bloom very gently on the surface, so that the flower head does not become waterlogged.

Choose a rose variety that has plenty of interest inside the flower, either with lots of petals like this one or with a pretty center and stamens.

Adjust the level of the water according to the height of the bowl and the angle from which it will be seen.

3 Continue adding blooms. The final number will depend on the size of the bowl, but there should be enough room so that they do not all crowd each other but can float freely.

On a hot night, you could add a few ice cubes to the water or perhaps a few drops of rose essential oil for added fragrance.

My Choice

An attractive bi-color with rather globular flowers with plenty of pink petals that are pale yellow on the reverse. This gives the unopened center of the bloom a yellow glow set amid the pink, open petals. The scent is superb, and the flowers good enough for exhibition. Growth is strong with plenty of branching, and disease resistance is good. Despite these merits it is not widely grown, which is a pity because it looks and smells good too.

Size	Height: 2½ ft. Spread: 2 ft.
Flowering	Early to late summer
Uses	Beds, exhibition
Scent	Strong fragrance

My Choice

Mischief

Mischief

This is an old variety – it has been around for over 30 years – but the reasons for planting it are as strong as when it was introduced. The profusion of coral-salmon blooms are beautifully shaped and rain-resistant, too. The color tends to be more "orangey" towards the end of summer. If you disbud the stems you can produce exhibition blooms, but most people prefer to enjoy the prolific display of smaller flowers for a general garden display. Prone to rust disease.

Size	Height: 2½ ft. Spread: 2 ft.
Flowering	Early to late summer
Uses	Beds, exhibition
Scent	Some scent

Bridesmaid's Rose and Ivy Circlet

A small circlet of fresh flowers is easy to make. Once you have mastered how to wire each flower and leaf, the rest is simple. Measure the child's head accurately and make the basic circlet, either with florist's wire or milliner's fabric-covered wire. Add a little extra to the circumference to allow for the thickness of the wires attaching flowers to the circlet. When complete, spray it with a fine mist of water to keep it fresh and then cover with damp tissue paper until required.

1 Cut off each rosebud and push wire through the fattest part of the stem. Twist the wire down and together, making a stem. Roll tape over the stem and down the length of wire.

2 With the underside of the leaf facing you, pierce each leaf with wire, twist and bring down to make a stem. Taping is not necessary. Prepare all the flowers and leaves you need.

3 Attach the roses and the rest of the leaves to the circlet using lengths of rose wire. Work round in one direction so that all the flowers face the same way.

A small-leaved variegated ivy makes the perfect foliage, as it is light and delicate but provides enough color contrast.

Attach each leaf to the circlet, using its own piece of wire.

If necessary, add more ivy leaves to fill in any large gaps or spaces in the final circlet.

4 Continue wiring the roses and ivy right round the circlet, alternating single larger roses with two or more miniature ones. Be sure to cover the circlet completely.

You could adapt this scheme for making a circlet to decorate a hat.

For added variety, choose larger and quite different roses.

Loving Memory

The strength of this variety lies in its large, well-formed blooms. The crimson-scarlet flowers are borne on vigorous, upright bushes, and the thick, dark green foliage keeps the plant well clothed so that the bush does not look too "twiggy". Its free-flowering nature combined with blooms of classic shape and reasonable fragrance makes this a special choice among red roses. The flowers are good enough to exhibit yet plentiful enough for bedding and for cutting.

Size Height: 3 ft. Spread: 2 ft.
Flowering Early to late summer
Uses Beds, exhibition
Scent Reasonably fragrant

Loving Memory

Michael Crawford

Michael Crawford

A recently introduced rose with large flowers of classic hybrid tea shape, soft orange inside with pale yellow on the reverse. The bushy plants are vigorous and appear to show good disease resistance, qualities now expected in modern varieties for general garden show. Although not especially fragrant, the attractive color combination should make it a popular bedding rose. Roses with attractive colors like this are also attractive if you have space for only a few plants.

Size Height: 2½ ft. Spread: 2 ft.
Flowering Early to late summer
Uses Bedding
Scent Reasonably fragrant

9

Victorian Rosebud Posy

S mall, hand-held posies, or "tussie-mussies" as they were once called, have been popular for centuries. Ideally they should contain strongly scented flowers to give the most pleasure. This small posy is made in organized rings of different colors and types of flowers, based on the kind of posy a Victorian girl might have carried.

1 Choose one beautiful rose bloom as the center starting point and hold it in one hand. Begin to build up a ring of carnations around it, using the other hand.

You can use rubber bands, florist wire or string to tie the bunch of flowers together.

2 Complete the white circle, then start a circle of alternate pink roses and paler carnations outside it, holding it steady in one hand. Tie it firmly after this stage.

Spray carnations or garden pinks have a sweet, spicy smell that blends well with the scent of roses.

3 Complete the posy with a final ring of love-in-a-mist or other appropriate flowers or foliage around the edge. Tie the whole bunch once again, winding wire rightly around the stems just below the flower heads.

4 The finished posy should be comfortable to hold. Do not be tempted to make it over large by bunching too many stems together.

L'Oreal Trophy

L'Oreal Trophy

This is a rose to chose for a specific purpose. It grows taller than most varieties, which makes it a good choice for a rose hedge with hybrid-tea-type blooms, or for massing in a large bed where tall varieties are easily accommodated. The long stems and attractively colored blooms make it a desirable cut flower. The color is a salmony-orange, and although the blooms are sometimes thinly petaled, this variety has a special charm that has won it many international awards.

Size	Height: 4 ft. Spread: 2½ ft.
Flowering	Early to late summer
Uses	Beds, borders, cutting, hedges
Scent	Some scent

Lovely Lady

Lovely Lady

Large shapely rose pink, very "full" flowers, ideal for bedding but suitable for exhibiting, too. It has the sort of flowers that look equally at home in a mixed border, as you might use many of the shrub roses. The strong, bushy growth and very large, glossy leaves make it a plant to admire as an isolated specimen as well as part of a massed display. Good disease resistance and a respectable fragrance are bonuses well worth having.

Size	Height: 2½ ft. Spread: 2 ft.
Flowering	Early to late summer
Uses	Beds, borders, exhibition
Scent	Reasonably fragrant

Rose and Fern Buttonhole

There are still certain formal occasions when people are expected to wear a lapel decoration and other less formal events where it simply adds style and a touch of fun. There is no need to order an expensive one from the flower shop as it is a very simple piece of floristry to put together yourself using home-grown flowers, as long as you choose varieties that will not wilt too quickly.

1 Choose a well-shaped, tightly closed bud and cut it off the main stem, leaving about 2 inches of stem below the bud.

2 Snip off a piece of leather fern to put behind the bud. The fern should be a little longer than the bud.

3 Wrap tape tightly around both stems, twisting and squeezing as you work down. Wind the tape back up the stem a little way and then cut off.

King's Ransom

A fter 30 years this bright and cheerful rose is still often recommended as one of the best pure yellows for garden display. The blooms are slow to fade and hold their color well, and the high-centered flowers have good traditional hybrid tea form. The variety flowers freely and stands up well to rain. The beautifully shaped buds make it a good choice for cutting. Growth is strong and upright, and disease resistance of the dark, glossy foliage is good.

Size	Height: 2½ ft. Spread: 2 ft.
Flowering	Early to late summer
Uses	Beds, cutting
Scent	Reasonably fragrant

King's Ransom

Lincoln Cathedral

Lincoln Cathedral

T his is one of those attractive roses with a color combination that it is difficult to pass by. The outer petals of the open flower are deep pink while the high-pointed center can be a color between peach and orange. The large blooms show up well against the dark glossy foliage, and the plant will enhance a mixed border as effectively as it will a dedicated rose bed. Unfortunately the scent does not live up to the promise of the flower.

Size	Height: 2½ ft. Spread 2 ft.
Flowering	Early to late summer
Uses	Beds, exhibition
Scent	Reasonably fragrant

7

Rose and Freesia Buttonhole

A garden rose makes an imaginative and scented lapel decoration compared with the dull and ubiquitous carnation. If you make it larger than a one- or two-flower version, you have a fine corsage suitable for a dressy suit, a ballgown or even a wedding hat.

Choose flowers that will stand this treatment, such as roses and freesias.

1 Choose a perfect bloom that is just at the point of opening from the bud stage and cut it away from the main stem, trimming away foliage and thorns.

2 Select a short trail of variegated ivy and cut away the lower leaves, leaving the stem clear. The ivy should be slightly longer than the rose stem to show behind the bloom.

3 Take another flower (here it is a freesia), and put it against the rose but extending slightly beyond it. Cut both stems to the same length.

4 Arrange the three stems of rose, freesia and ivy in your hand, with the rose at the front. If possible, hold the flowers against the clothes that are to be worn.

5 Bind the stems closely with green tape, working from the flower heads down the stems. Cover the cut stem ends and bring the tape back up, squeezing it tightly before cutting it.

6 Attach an extra long, fine dressmaker's pin from behind the fabric or put through a buttonhole and pin securely under the lapel.

Just Joey

This rose has been a favorite for years, many gardeners being attracted by its distinctive color coupled with a strong scent. The coppery-orange petals, almost veined red, have an attractive, frilled appearance. The blooms are well set off by the bronze-green foliage. The flowers are not large, but make up for this by being so freely produced. This vigorous grower has good disease resistance and can be relied upon to put in a good performance.

Size	Height: 2½ ft. Spread: 2 ft.
Flowering	Early to late summer
Uses	Beds, exhibition
Scent	Strong fragrance

Just Joey

Keepsake

Keepsake

This is a rose to grow for its color alone, which looks marvellous cut for summer arrangements or covering a plant in the garden. The color is sometimes described as cherry-pink, but whichever words you choose to describe it you are sure to be impressed by the color intensity of this pink rose. It is a vigorous, upright grower, and there are always plenty of leaves to act as a green foil for the perfectly formed flowers.

Size	Height: 2½ ft. Spread: 2 ft.
Flowering	Early to late summer
Uses	Beds, cutting
Scent	Sweetly fragrant

Lilac and Apricot Bouquet

Here a subtle mixture of lilac, sweet peas and statice is combined with warm apricot roses to make a sweetly scented bunch. The easiest way to make a bouquet like this, whether large or small, is to make it in your hand, building up flower by flower until it is complete and full. Finish it off with a bow in a matching color.

3 Continue adding blooms, mixing the colors and varieties as much as possible and working round evenly. Hold the bunch as tightly as possible.

4 When the bouquet is finished, cut the stems to make them all the same length and secure the whole thing with a rubber band or wire.

5 Lay the bunch of flowers down and wrap a ribbon around the stems, covering the rubber band. Knot tightly and tie an attractive bow.

Use good quality ribbon to make the bouquet more of a special gift.

The recipient can remove the ribbon before standing the bouquet in water.

At this stage, do not worry that the stems are different lengths.

1 If the roses are floribunda types, begin by separating them into single stems and clean off the thorns and leaves.

Dividing up a multi-stemmed rose will determine the length of the finished posy.

2 First hold one or two stems tightly in one hand and add another flower with the other hand.

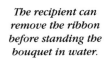

6 The finished bouquet is pretty enough for a bridesmaid to carry. Try making different color versions.

Grandpa Dickson

This rose was introduced more than a quarter of a century ago, but it still has a following and nurseries still grow it. Any rose that old which still sells despite competition from breeders in the intervening years has qualities. This is quite simply a good all-rounder: it looks good in rose beds, can be grown to a standard adequate for the show bench, and it makes a good cut rose, too. The almost pale green buds open to pale yellow flushed pink.

Size	Height: 2½ ft. Spread: 2 ft.
Flowering	Early to late summer
Uses	Beds, cutting, exhibition
Scent	Some scent

Ingrid Bergman

Grandpa Dickson

Ingrid Bergman

One of the best red hybrid teas for bedding. The rich, deep red flowers seem to have an intensity of color that many other reds lack, especially as they age. The flower shape is good and the blooms are carried on strong single stems. The upright growth habit and taller than average height make it a candidate for a rose hedge where you want to use a hybrid tea rose. It has above average disease resistance and performs well in all weathers.

Size	Height: 3 ft. Spread: 2 ft.
Flowering	Early to late summer
Uses	Beds, borders, hedges
Scent	Strong fragrance

Traditional Wreath of Striped Roses

Garlands or wreaths are a good way of making the most of a few special flowers. The easiest way is to use a ready-made foam ring. Roses are ideal in wreaths along with some other foliage or plant material to work as a filler. Keep the finished wreath moist with an occasional fine spray of water.

You will need a loop of wire if you intend to hang the wreath vertically.

Follow the manufacturer's instructions on soaking the foam so that it is neither too wet or too dry.

77

1 Make a small loop round the ring with garden wire. Soak the ring in water before filling it with flowers. Work with the ring held vertically or horizontally, whichever is comfortable for you.

2 Using short stems of gypsophila as a filler, work round the ring, (above) covering it completely.

3 Next, begin to add short stems of dianthus, spacing them evenly (left) throughout the gypsophila.

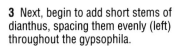

4 Add the roses, filling the spaces between the dianthus to create a densely textured effect.

Fragrant Cloud

The name says it all. This is a variety to include if fragrance is important. Despite being over 30 years old, it holds its own with modern varieties when it comes to scent. The large, well-shaped blooms are coral-scarlet, shifting towards crimson with age, and produced almost as freely as flowers on a floribunda. Its scent and free-blooming habit also make it a good choice as a cut flower. It is a robust grower, yet still compact.

Size   Height: 2½ ft. Spread: 2 ft.
Flowering Early to late summer
Uses   Beds, cutting
Scent   Exceptional fragrance

Freedom

The strengths of this variety lie in its strong yellow color that is slow to fade, and its resistance to diseases such as blackspot. It shows the vigor typical of many modern varieties, yet the plants remain compact, qualities that make it ideal for bedding. The really intense yellow, well-formed flowers are freely produced and have all the qualities of a well-shaped hybrid tea rose. Certainly one of the brightest yellow hybrid teas, and not easily spoiled by rain.

Size   Height: 2½ ft. Spread: 2 ft.
Flowering Early to late summer
Uses   Beds
Scent   Reasonably fragrant

Fragrant Cloud

Freedom

4

Candlesticks Adorned with Miniature Roses

Roses always look good used as table decorations, and partnered with candlelight they look even better. Here, two ordinary recycled glass candlesticks have been given a glamorous treatment with a ring of foam round them to hold small red roses and sprigs of fern leaf.

1 Cut small pieces of foam about 1 in thick. Make a hole right through the foam by pushing down with the candle.

Put the foliage in place as a filler and to provide a contrast to the flowers.

Most candlesticks have a suitable "drip tray" on which you can support the foam ring.

2 Mark out a circle round the hole, about 3 ½ inches across, depending on the size of candles and holder. Cut it out with a knife and soak the foam.

3 Prepare the roses and foliage by separating the flowers from the bunches and cutting the stems short. Do the same with the foliage.

4 Place the foam ring on the candlestick and push the candle through. Use small pieces of florist fixing tape to secure it if necessary.

5 Once you have a base of green foliage, begin to add the roses and buds, working round the ring.

6 The finished decoration could be a matching pair of candlesticks or a single decoration. One for each guest.

Cherry Brandy

This is a good bedding rose as some of the flowers are produced in clusters as well as singly. The color is bright salmon-orange, approaching pure orange, making a bed of them bright and colorful even from a distance. The classically-shaped blooms are well set off by the healthy, mid-green foliage. The upright growth and long, firm stems, coupled with bright glossy foliage, make it an attractive cut-flower variety too.

Size	Height: 2½ ft. Spread: 2 ft.
Flowering	Early to late summer
Uses	Beds, cutting
Scent	Reasonably fragrant

Dawn Chorus

Cherry Brandy

Dawn Chorus

One of the best recent introductions, this variety has classic, high-centered hybrid tea flowers with a charming color blend that mixes tangerine with a strong hint of golden yellow at the base. The charming combination is eye-catching for individual blooms and if viewed *en mass* from a distance. It also flowers with the profusion of a floribunda. The young foliage is attractively copper-tinted. The compact plants look in place even in a small garden.

Size	Height: 2½ ft. Spread: 2 ft.
Flowering	Early to late summer
Uses	Beds, exhibition
Scent	Reasonably fragrant

A Hatful of Roses

This simple rose decoration transforms an everyday straw hat into something special for a grand occasion or summer wedding. Choose roses in a color to match your clothes.

This is "Aloha", a climbing rose with an old-fashioned look and beautiful, rich color.

1 Choose two perfect matching blooms and trim, leaving about 3 inches of stem and leaf. Wrap tape round the stem, making sure that you enclose the cut end. Put the two roses together, one just above the other, and bind them together with tape to make one stem.

2 Position the roses on the hat at the base of the crown on one side. Using fine rose wire, attach the rose stems to the hat by threading the wire right through the straw inside the crown and out again. Twist the wire tightly round the stems a few times and neatly cut off any extra wire.

3 Fold a chiffon scarf round the base of the crown or wrap a wide ribbon round it to cover the rose stems. Knot or tie into a bow at the back of the hat.

Alpine Sunset

An aptly named rose, as the creamy-yellow blooms are flushed with the sort of peach-pink you sometimes see in sunsets. A sturdy grower, it flowers freely and makes a reliable garden plant, possessing that all-important quality of good disease resistance. Unfortunately it tends to produce its flowers in a series of separate flushes rather than continually. The color, fragrance and strong stems make it a good variety to use for cutting.

Size	Height: 2 ft. Spread: 2 ft.
Flowering	Early to late summer
Uses	Beds, cutting, exhibition
Scent	Strong fragrance

Alpine Sunset

Blessings

For a reliable pink rose with a good shape and scent, "Blessings" is an excellent choice. The soft coral-pink blooms are mainly produced singly but also in trusses (exposing its ancestry – the famous "Queen Elizabeth" was one parent), on healthy bushes with strong, rather upright, growth. The flowers are produced continuously – it is seldom without a flower during the summer, making it a particularly reliable and impressive bedding variety.

Size	Height: 3 ft. Spread: 2 ft.
Flowering	Early to late summer
Uses	Beds
Scent	Reasonably fragrant

Layered Rose Potpourri

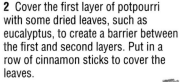

A nother way to exploit the decorative possibilities of roses is to dry them and layer up potpourri mixtures in a plain glass tank and decorate the top with whole dried roses. The petal mixture can be simply decorative or you can make a proper potpourri with essential oils and fixatives.

1 Put a layer of potpourri at the bottom of the glass tank and press it down well. With care, you can position the best pieces and prettiest flowers against the front of the glass.

This mixture is a home-made potpourri of roses and other dried garden flowers and leaves, including tulip petals, hibiscus and peony petals.

Cinnamon sticks also add another scent to the display.

2 Cover the first layer of potpourri with some dried leaves, such as eucalyptus, to create a barrier between the first and second layers. Put in a row of cinnamon sticks to cover the leaves.

3 Add another layer of a different color potpourri and then decorate the whole of the top with complete dried roses from side to side.

4 The finished arrangement is ideal as a bedroom decoration. Stand it away from direct bright sunlight, otherwise the colors will quickly fade.

Eucalyptus leaves provide interesting contrast and divide up the different layers.

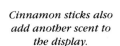
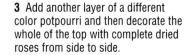

Alec's Red

One of the best red hybrid tea roses. The well-formed classic hybrid tea-shaped and large globular profile coupled with an intense cherry red color is a combination that keeps this variety popular, despite having been introduced over 20 years ago. Good scent, sturdy growth, strong stems, and good rain resistance are other plus points. Disease resistance is also an attribute that makes this a rose to grow in the modern garden.

Size	Height: 2½ ft. Spread: 2 ft.
Flowering	Early to late summer
Uses	Beds, exhibition
Scent	Strong fragrance

Above and below: Alec's Red

Alexander

The brilliant vermilion color makes this rose stand out, even from a distance. It is even brighter and more luminous than the other old favorite "Super Star" (one of its parents). Although the blooms are only medium-sized there are plenty of them, freely produced on tall, well-branched plants. Its size makes it a good choice to grow in a mixed border, and even as a hedge if you want one with hybrid tea blooms. A weakness is its mediocre scent.

Size	Height: 4 ft. Spread: 2 ft.
Flowering	Early to late summer
Uses	Beds, borders, hedging
Scent	Reasonably fragrant

Rose Varieties

Classifying Roses

Some years ago the World Federation of Rose Societies introduced a new classification to describe better the groups into which we place some of our most common varieties. The traditional hybrid teas became known as large-flowered bush roses. The floribundas became known as cluster-flowered bush roses. These terms are now widely used by rose enthusiasts, but most gardeners and rose catalogs still use the long-established terms of hybrid tea and floribunda. For that reason, we have used these terms in this book.

Many modern floribunda varieties have large, well-formed blooms that resemble hybrid tea roses, and it can sometimes be difficult to decide to which group a variety belongs. In these borderline cases we have adopted the classification most often used.

Much breeding now goes into producing more compact floribunda roses, and the dwarfest of these are sometimes listed as "patio roses". You will find roses suitable for patio beds and pots suggested in both floribundas and miniatures.

Describing Colors

Describing the color of any flower can be difficult, but it is a particular problem with roses. Flowers that open yellow may turn white when they are fully out, and a variety that looks pink as the buds unfurl may become peach or orange fully, opened.

Many floribundas have multi-colored heads because they contain flowers at different stages of development. Reds and yellows especially may fade with age or exposure to sunshine. Soil, temperature, sun or shade can all affect the flower color.

With one picture it is possible to represent the bloom only at one point in time, but the captions suggest the colors you are most likely to see in the mature flower before it begins to age.

Hybrid Teas